Goodwill's

MOST COMMON ERRORS IN ENGLISH

By

Madan Sood

M.A. English (Lit.)

(Formerly of Indian Air Force)

GOODWILL PUBLISHING HOUSE®

New Delhi

Published by :
GOODWILL PUBLISHING HOUSE
B-3, Rattan Jyoti, 18, Rajendra Place,
New Delhi-110008 (INDIA)
Ph. : 25750801, 25820556
Fax : 91-11-25764396
Web : goodwillpublishinghouse.com
E-mail : goodwillpub@vsnl.net

© Publishers

No part of this book may be reproduced, stored in a retrieval system or transmitted in any form or by any means, mechanical, photocopying or otherwise without the written permission of the publisher. Anybody doing so shall face legal action.

Laser Typeset at : Computer Corner, New Delhi

Printed at Kumar Offset Printers, Delhi-110092

Contents

PREFACE

There is no denying the fact that the knowledge of English language is becoming an inevitable necessity each day. No one can claim to be an expert in any language unless he has mastered the rules of grammar of that language.

Inspite of the best efforts, the students and other scholars are unable to speak and write flawless English and the fact can invariably be attributed to their lack of knowledge of English grammar.

This book - *Most Common Errors in English* - incorporates all the chapters of grammar where there is a possibility of errors cropping in. At the end of each chapter clues (answers) have been provided for each wrong sentence, thereby enabling the reader to ascertain the cause of inaccuracy of a particular sentence.

Chapters - Tenses, Sequence of Tenses, Narration, Adverbs, Adjectives, Articles, Punctuation, Letter Writing, Idioms and Phrases, Prepositions, Agreement of the Verb with the Subject, Paronyms, Homonyms, Spellings, Question tags and Short Answers and some miscellaneous exercises - have been incorporated, so that the reader can learn the rules of grammar besides knowing the flaws which invariably crop in while writing or speaking English. I hope that this book will prove to be a boon not only for students of all standards but for a general reader also.

— Madan Sood

1

Errors in the Use of Tenses

Tenses may be defined as that form of a verb which shows the time and the state of an action or event. Carefully study the following table of Tenses of the verb of love :

	Present Tense	
	Active	*Passive*
Simple	I love	I am loved
Continuous	I am loving	I am being loved
Perfect	I have loved	I have been loved
Perfect continuous	I have been loving	
	Past Tense	
	Active	*Passive*
Simple	I loved	I was loved
Continuous	I was loving	I was being loved
Perfect	I had loved	I had been loved
Perfect continuous	I had been loving	
	Future Tense	
	Active	*Passive*
Simple	I shall love	I shall be loved
Continuous	I shall be loving	
Perfect	I shall have loved	I shall have been loved
Perfect continuous	I shall have been loving	

It will be seen that there are twelve tenses in the Active Voice and eight in the passive. Below are given sentences of different tenses showing errors generally committed in the use of tenses :

1. ✘ She take vegetarian food.
   ✔ She takes vegetarian food.
2. ✘ I takes bath every day.
   ✔ I take bath every day.
3. ✘ This newspaper appear twice a week.
   ✔ This newspaper appears twice a week.
4. ✘ We plays cricket on Sundays.
   ✔ We play cricket on Sundays.
5. ✘ Boys makes a lot of noise here.
   ✔ Boys make a lot of noise here.
6. ✘ The sun rise in the east.
   ✔ The sun rises in the east.
7. ✘ He run fast.
   ✔ He runs fast.
8. ✘ All men worships God.
   ✔ All men worship God.
9. ✘ The judge punish the accused.
   ✔ The judge punishes the accused.
10. ✘ He don't come here regularly.
    ✔ He doesn't come here regularly.
11. ✘ This dog do not barks loudly.
    ✔ This dog does not bark loudly.
12. ✘ Do she speak softly?
    ✔ Does she speak softly?
13. ✘ Does you play cricket?
    ✔ Do you play cricket?

14. ✗ She does not knows you.
    ✓ She does not know you.
15. ✗ She does not speaks fluent English.
    ✓ She does not speak fluent English.
16. ✗ Why don't he come to office in time?
    ✓ Why doesn't he come to office in time?
17. ✗ Where does he lives?
    ✓ Where does he live?

18. ✗ Which book did you wrote?
    ✓ Which book did you write?
19. ✗ When does you get up?
    ✓ When do you get up?
20. ✗ Who does teach you English?
    ✓ Who teaches you English?
21. ✗ What does bring you here?
    ✓ What brings you here?

CLUES

(i) All the above sentences are Simple Present.

(ii) In simple present tense present form of the verb is used.

(iii) When the subject is third person singular Number (he, she, it), 's' or 'es' is used with the main verb.

(iv) For making negative and interrogative sentences, 'do' or 'does' is used.

(v) 'Does' is used when the subject is Third Person Singular Number (he, she, it), and 'do' is used with all other subjects.

(vi) When 'does' is used 's' or 'es' is not used with the main verb.

1. ✗ I is learning English.

   ✓ I am learning English.

2. ✗ The teacher are teaching the class.

   ✓ The teacher is teaching the class.

3. ✗ The boys are play cricket in the park.

   ✓ The boys are playing cricket in the park.

4. ✗ The birds is not singing.

   ✓ The bird is not singing.

5. ✗ The gardener is water the plants.

   ✓ The gardener is watering the plants.

6. ✗ The pilot are flying a jet aeroplane.

   ✓ The pilot is flying a jet aeroplane.

7. ✗ Is she listen to the music?

   ✓ Is she listening to the music?

8. ✗ The woman is not cut the grass.

   ✓ The woman is not cutting the grass.

9. ✗ Are you go to market?

   ✓ Are you going to market?

10. ✗ Where are you go?

    ✓ Where are you going?

11. ✗ Which book are you read ?

    ✓ Which book are you reading ?

12. ✗ Isn't his parents watching T.V.?

    ✓ Aren't his parents watching T.V.?

CLUES

(i) All the above sentences belong to Present Continuous Tense.

(ii) The auxiliary 'is' or 'are' or 'am' is used - 'I' takes 'am', all plural subjects take 'are' and third person singular number takes 'is'.

(iii) Present form of the main verb + ing is used.

1. ✘ The gardener has water the plants.
   ✔ The gardener has watered the plants.
2. ✘ The child have broken the toy.
   ✔ The child has broken the toy.
3. ✘ Mother have cooked the food.
   ✔ Mother has cooked the food.
4. ✘ The doctors has examined the patients.
   ✔ The doctors have examined the patients.
5. ✘ Who have taught you this lesson?
   ✔ Who has taught you this lesson?
6. ✘ When have he taken his lunch?
   ✔ When has he taken his lunch?
7. ✘ Where have he went? 
   ✔ Where has he gone?
8. ✘ My father haven't gone to office.
   ✔ My father hasn't gone to office.
9. ✘ The boy has not completed their work yet.
   ✔ The boys have not completed their work yet.
10. ✘ Have he read Shakespeare's Hamlet?
    ✔ Has he read Shakespeare's Hamlet?
11. ✘ Has he return your money?
    ✔ Has he returned your money?
12. ✘ The Britishers quitted India in 1947.

✔ The Britishers quit India in 1947.

13. ✘ The All India Radio has already broadcasted this programme.

    ✔ The all India Radio has already broadcast this programme.

14. ✘ The gardener has cutted many saplings.

    ✔ The gardener has cut many saplings.

15. ✘ Where has you kept my books?

    ✔ Where have you kept my books?

CLUES

(i) All the above sentences belong to Present Perfect Tense.

(ii) In present perfect tense, the auxiliary 'has' or 'have', is used.

(iii) 'Has' is used with the subjects which are third person singular number (he , she, it)

(iv) 'Have' is used with all the remaining subjects.

(v) Past participle form of the main verb is used.

1. ✘ I am working since morning.

   ✔ I have been working since morning.

2. ✘ The boys have been play for two hours.

   ✔ The boys have been playing for two hours.

3. ✘ The girls have been dancing since two hours.

   ✔ The girls have been dancing for two hours.

4. ✘ The teacher has been teaching the class since forty minutes.

✔ The teacher has been teaching the class for forty minutes.

5. ✘ Mother have been cooking for morning.

   ✔ Mother has been cooking since morning.

6. ✘ Sita haven't been knitting the sweater since two months.

   ✔ Sita hasn't been knitting the sweater for two months.

7. ✘ Radha has been dance since morning.

   ✔ Radha has been dancing since morning.

8. ✘ Your father have not been working here since a long time.

   ✔ Your father has not been working here for a long time.

9. ✘ Has your parents been waiting for a long time?

   ✔ Have your parents been waiting for a long time?

10. ✘ He has been working in this office since 10 years.

    ✔ He has been working in this office for 10 years.

11. ✘ Has he been sleeping for 3 p.m?

    ✔ Has he been sleeping since 3 p.m.?

12. ✘ Has you been driving for ten hours?

    ✔ Have you been driving for ten hours?

CLUES

(i) All the above sentences belong to Present Perfect Continuous Tense.

(ii) In this tense, the auxiliary 'has been' or 'have been' is used.

(iii) 'Has been' is used with the subjects which are third person singular number. 'Have been' is used with all the remaining subjects.

(iv) Present form of the main verb + ing is used.

(v) 'Since' is used to denote **point of time** and 'for' is used to denote **period of time**.

1. ✗ I write him a letter yesterday.
   ✔ I wrote him a letter yesterday.
2. ✗ I have read this news yesterday.
   ✔ I read this news yesterday.
3. ✗ I have seen him in the party last week.
   ✔ I saw him in the party last week.
4. ✗ A film star inaugurate the function.
   ✔ A film star inaugurated the function.

5. ✗ I did not went to school yesterday.
   ✔ I did not go to school yesterday.
6. ✗ The principal did not gave a long speech.
   ✔ The principal did not give a long speech.
7. ✗ Why didn't you helped him?
   ✔ Why didn't you help him?

8. ✗ Did the Prime Minister planted a sapling ?

   ✔ Did the Prime Minister plant a sapling ?

9. ✗ Did the Britishers quitted India in 1947 ?

   ✔ Did the Britishers quit India in 1947 ?

10. ✗ Did you attended the function yesterday ?

    ✔ Did you attend the function yesterday ?

11. ✗ Where did you kept my money ?

    ✔ Where did you keep my money ?

12. ✗ She did not threatened me.

    ✔ She did not threaten me.

13. ✗ When did you came back ?

    ✔ When did you come back ?

14. ✗ She did not knew the traffic rules.

    ✔ She did not know the traffic rules

15. ✗ Why did you disobeyed the traffic rules ?

    ✔ Why did you disobey the traffic rules ?

CLUES

(i) All the above sentences belong to Simple Past Tense.

(ii) In this tense Past form of the verb is used.

(iii) Auxiliary 'Did' is used to make negative and interrogative sentences of Past Simple Tense.

(iv) Present form of the verb is used in this tense with Negative and Interrogative sentences (when 'did' has already been used)

1. ✗ Where were the girls dance ?

   ✔ Where were the girls dancing ?

2. ✗ The boy were watching the cricket match.

   ✔ The boy was watchinr the cricket match.

3. ✗ Was the washermen washing the clothes ?

✓ Were the washermen washing the clothes ?

4. ✗ She was not make the clay models.

✓ She was not making the clay models.

5. ✗ Was you sweeping the floor ?

✓ Were you sweeping the floor ?

CLUES

(i) All the above sentences belong to Past Continuous Tense.

(ii) Auxiliary 'was' is used with singular subjects and Auxiliary 'were' is used with plural subjects.

(iii) Present form of the verb + ing is used.

1. ✗ I had completed my work when my father had came.

✓ I had completed my work when my father came.

2. ✗ The fishermen caught the catch when the storm had come.

✓ The fishermen had caught the catch when the storm came.

3. ✗ The patient had not recovered when the doctor come.

✓ The patient had not recovered when the doctor came.

4. ✗ The gardener not planted the saplings before we reached there.

✓ The gardener had not planted the saplings before we reached there.

5. ✗ The pilot baled out before the engine had caught fire.

✓ The pilot had baled out before the engine caught fire.

6. ✗ Had the girls sang the song when the chief guest arrived?

✔ Had the girls sung the song when the chief guest arrived?

7. ✘ Had you complete your work when the teacher came?

   ✔ Had you completed your work when the teacher came?

8. ✘ They dismissed the employee when the hearing had started.

   ✔ They had dismissed the employee when the hearing started.

9. ✘ I not entered the house when the rain started.

   ✔ I had not entered the house when the rain started.

10. ✘ You had not wrote your answers when the principal came.

    ✔ You had not written your answers when the principal came.

CLUES

(i) All the above sentences belong to Past Perfect Tense.

(ii) This tense is used to describe that action in the past which was completed before another action of the past.

(iii) The action which happened earlier than the other action in the past, is conveyed through a clause of past perfect tense and the action which happened later, is put in a clause of past simple tense.

(iv) Auxiliary 'had' is used with all the subjects.

(v) Past participle form of the main verb is used.

(vi) Another clause of past simple tense is used to show the action which happened later.

1. ✘ I had been studying in Doon Public School for 1985.

   ✔ I had been studying in Doon Public School since 1985.

2. ✘ We had been wait for the bus for one hour.

   ✔ We had been waiting for the bus for one hour.

3. ✘ The girls had been learning their lessons since long.
   ✔ The girls had been learning their lessons for long.

4. ✘ The labourers had not been work since morning.
   ✔ The labourers had not been working since morning.
5. ✘ Had the cashier been counting the cash for morning?
   ✔ Had the cashier been counting the cash since morning?
6. ✘ You had been not playing for a long time.
   ✔ You had not been playing for a long time.

7. ✘ Had you been not learning guitar since one year?
   ✔ Had you not been learning guitar for one year?
8. ✘ The students had been not doing their home work for one hour.
   ✔ The students had not been doing their home work for one hour.

CLUES

(i) All the above sentences belong to Past Perfect Continuous Tense.

(ii) In this tense 'had been' is used with all the subjects.

(iii) Present form of the verb + ing is used.

(iv) 'Since' or 'for' is used.

1. ✘ She shall do her home work.
   ✔ She will do her home work.
2. ✘ The hawker shall sell the wares.
   ✔ The hawker will sell the wares.

3. ✘ I shall not met him tomorrow.

   ✔ I shall not meet him tomorrow.

4. ✘ Mother will brought milk.

   ✔ Mother will bring milk.

5. ✘ They shall help us in our difficulties.

   ✔ They will help us in our difficulties.

CLUES

(i) The above sentences belong to Future Simple Tense.

(ii) In this tense, the auxiliary 'shall' or 'will' is used.

(iii) 'Shall' is used with first person singular number and plural number, (I, we).

(iv) 'Will' is used with all other subjects (you, he, she, it, they)

Note : 'Will' can also be used with first person singular number and plural number and 'shall' can also be used with all other subjects (you, he, she, it, they). However, that use is restricted to Modal Auxiliaries.

1. ✘ The boys shall be doing their home work.

   ✔ The boys will be doing their home work.

2. ✘ Father shall be reading the newspaper.

   ✔ Father will be reading the newspaper.

3. ✘ The hawker will be sell the newspapers.

   4 The hawker will be selling the newspapers.

4. ✘ The girls will be not doing rehearsal for the function.

   ✔ The girls will not be doing rehearsal for the function.

5. ✘ Will the gardener watering the plants?

   ✔ Will the gardener be watering the plants?

6. ✗ Will be the doctor examining the patient?

   ✔ Will the doctor be examining the patient?

7. ✗ Will you be watch T.V.?

   ✔ Will you be watching T.V.?

8. ✗ We shall be not taking our food then.

   ✔ We shall not be taking our food then.

CLUES

(i) The above sentences belong to Future Continuous tense.

(ii) In this tense 'shall be' is used with first person singular and plural Number (I, we), and 'will be' is used with all other subjects (persons)

(iii) Present form of the verb + ing is used.

1. ✗ The train will have leave the platform.

   ✔ The train will have left the platform.

2. ✗ The players will have withdrew the stumps before sunset.

   ✔ The players will have withdrawn the stumps before sunset.

3. ✗ The principal will have not completed his speech.

✓ The principal will not have completed his speech.

4. ✗ I shall not have took my dinner by 8 p.m.

✓ I shall not have taken my dinner by 8 p.m.

5. ✗ Will the chief guest inaugurated the function?

✓ Will the chief guest have inaugurated the function?

6. ✗ The aeroplane will have not took off.

✓ The aeroplane will not have taken off.

CLUES

(i) The above sentences belong to Future Perfect Tense.

(ii) In this tense 'shall have' is used with First Person Singular Number and First Person Plural Number (I, we), and 'will have' is used with all the remaining subjects (persons).

(iii) Past participle form of the main verb is used.

1. ✗ She shall have been cooking since half an hour.

✓ She will have been cooking for half an hour.

2. ✗ The driver will have been not driving the bus for twelve hours.

✓ The driver will not have been driving the bus for twelve hours.

3. ✘ The spectators will have been watch the match for five hours.

   ✔ The spectators will have been watching the match for five hours.

4. ✘ Will have they been working since morning?

   ✔ Will they have been working since morning?

5. ✘ Shall have the doctors been diagnosing the patients for a long time?

   ✔ Will the doctors have been diagnosing the patients for a long time?

6. ✘ He will have not been working since afternoon.

   ✔ He will not have been working since afternoon.

CLUES

(i) The above sentences are Future Perfect Continuous tenses.

(ii) In this tense, 'shall have been' is used with First Person Singular Number and Plural Number (I, we) and 'will have been' is used with all other persons (subjects).

(iii) Present form of the verb + ing is used.

(iv) 'Since' or 'for' is used.

2

Sequence of Tenses

The sequence is the principle according to which a sentence follows another within a long sentence. Because of the lack of proper relationship in sequence of tenses, many errors are committed in spoken and written English.

The verb of the principal clause is followed by the verb in the subordinate clause in relation to time.

A verb in the past tense in the main clause is invariably followed by a verb in the same tense in the subordinate clause.

A subordinate clause is a group of words having a subject and a predicate and joined to the main clause by a conjunction. However, there are two exceptions to this rule. First, a past tense in the main or principal clause may be followed by a present tense in the subordinate clause if it expresses a universal truth and secondly, when the subordinate clause is introduced by than. Errors crop in when these rules are not followed. Therefore, the readers are advised to carefully study the following errors.

1. ✘ He hinted that he wants leave.
   ✔ He hinted that he wanted leave.
2. ✘ He said that his father feels better.
   ✔ He said that his father felt better.
3. ✘ The police found out that he is guilty.

✔ The police found out that he was guilty.

4. ✘ I saw that the clock has stopped.

   ✔ I saw that the clock had stopped.

5. ✘ She said that she will come.

   ✔ She said that she would come.

6. ✘ We never thought that we shall see him again.

   ✔ We never thought that we would see him again.

7. ✘ We took care that they shall not hear us.

   ✔ We took care that they should not hear us.

8. ✘ We climbed higher that we may get a better view.

   ✔ We climbed higher that we might get a better view.

9. ✘ He worked hard that he may succeed.

   ✔ He worked hard that he might succeed.

CLUES

(i) The Sequence of Tenses is the principle in accordance with which the Tense of the verb in a Subordinate Clause follows the tense of the verb in the principal clause (Sequence is connected with the Latin verb *sequor,* follow).

(ii) The Sequence of Tenses applies chiefly to Adverb Clauses of Purpose and Noun Clauses.

(iii) A Past Tense in the principal clause is followed by a Past Tense in the subordinate clause as is shown in the above sentences.

10. ✘ Newton discovered that the force of gravitation made apples fall.

    ✔ Newton discovered that the force of gravitation makes apples fall.

11. ✗ Galileo maintained that the earth moved round the sun.

✔ Galileo maintained that the earth moves round the sun.

12. ✗ Euclid proved that the three angles of a triangle were equal to two right angles.

✔ Euclid proved that the three angles of a triangle are equal to two right angles.

13. ✗ The teacher said that honesty was the best policy.

✔ The teacher said that honesty is the best policy.

CLUES

(i) There are two exceptions to the rule mentioned in the earlier clues.

(ii) A Past Tense in the principal clause may be followed by a Present Tense in the subordinate clause when the subordinate clause expresses a universal truth.

(iii) When the subordinate clause is introduced by 'than', even if there is a past tense in principal clause, it may be followed by any tense required by the sense in the subordinate clause. See the following examples.

14. ✔ She liked you better than she likes me.

15. ✔ You helped him more than you help your own children.

16. ✔ He then saw me oftener than he sees me now.

17. ✔ You valued your friendship more than you value mine.

CLUES

A Present or Future Tense in principal clause may be followed by any tense required by the sense in the subordinate clauses. See the following examples.

18. ✔ She thinks that he is there.

19. ✔ She thinks that he was there.

20. ✔ She thinks that he will be there.

21. ✔ She will think that he is there.

22. ✔ She will think that he was there.

23. ✔ She will think that she will be there.

CLUES

In the sentences where the subordinate clause denotes purpose, if the verb in the principal clause is present or future, the verb in the subordinate clause must be present. See the following examples.

24. ✘ I eat that I might live.

    ✔ I eat that I may live.

25. ✘ I shall nurse him so that he could live.

    ✔ I shall nurse him so that he can live.

3

Wrong Use of Adjectives

Adjectives are words which tell us something about other words, that is, nouns. With the use of adjectives, beauty, colour and meaning are added to the nouns. We commit errors in the use of adjectives because we either confuse them with the adverbs or nouns.

We should always keep in mind the basic difference between adjectives and adverbs. While comparing two persons or things, the comparative degree is used. When comparison involves more than two persons or things, the superlative degree of adjective is used. Study the following sentences carefully to understand the correct usage of adjectives :

1. ✗ The poor man had seen happy days.

   ✔ The poor man had seen happier days.

2. ✗ Hunger is the better sauce.

   ✔ Hunger is the best sauce.

3. ✗ A live ass is strong than a dead lion.

   ✔ A live ass is stronger than a dead lion.

4. ✘ Soloman was one of the wiser men.
   ✔ Soloman was one of the wisest men.
5. ✘ Her simple word is as better as an oath.
   ✔ Her simple word is as good as an oath.
6. ✘ Hunger is the well sauce.
   ✔ Hunger is the best sauce
7. ✘ There was not the slighter excuse for it.
   ✔ There was not the slightest excuse for it.
8. ✘ My knife is sharpest than yours.
   ✔ My knife is sharper than yours.
9. ✘ Smaller people love to talk of greater men.
   ✔ Small people love to talk of great men.
10. ✘ Open rebuke is good than secret love.
    ✔ Open rebuke is better than secret love.
11. ✘ John is the idler boy in the class.
    ✔ John is the idlest boy in boy in the class.
12. ✘ I promise you a fare hearing.
    ✔ I promise you a fair hearing.
13. ✘ There is more to be said on both sides.
    ✔ There is much to be said on both sides.
14. ✘ I gave the boys more wholesome advice.
    ✔ I gave the boys much wholesome advice.
15. ✘ She thinks she is wise than her father.
    ✔ She thinks she is wiser than her father.
16. ✘ England has the larger fleet in the world.
    ✔ England has the largest fleet in the world.
17. ✘ Lead is heaviest than any other metal.
    ✔ Lead is heavier than any other metal.

18. ✘ We congratulated him on his well fortune.

✔ We congratulated him on his good fortune.

19. ✘ The longer lane has a turning.

✔ The longest lane has a turning.

20. ✘ He is latter than I expected.

✔ He is later than I expected.

21. ✘ I have not heard the last news.

✔ I have not heard the latest news.

22. ✘ The later chapters of this book are lacking in interest.

✔ The latter chapters of this book are lacking in interest.

23. ✘ The later chapter is carelessly written.

✔ The last chapter is carelessly written.

24. ✘ Ours is the latter house in the street.

✔ Ours is the last house in the street.

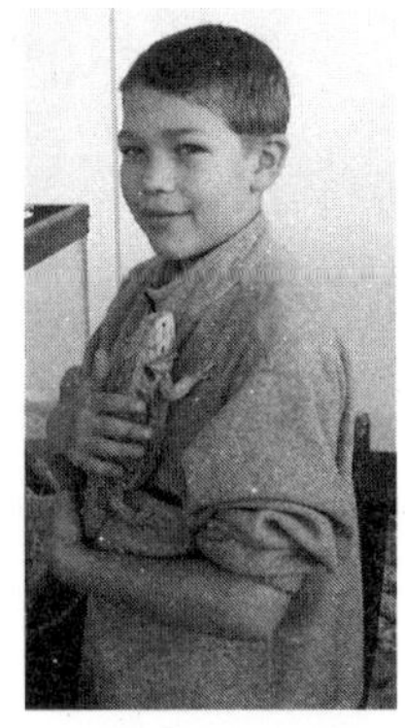

25. ✘ John is my older brother.

✔ John is my elder brother.

26. ✘ He is elder than his sister.

✔ He is older than his sister.

27. ✘ Tom is the older boy in the eleven.

✔ Tom is the oldest boy in the eleven.

28. ✘ This is the older temple in Kolkata.

✔ This is the oldest temple in Kolkata.

29. ✘ Kolkata is further from the equator than Colombo.

✔ Kolkata is farther from the equator than Colombo.

30. ✘ After this he made no farther remarks.

✔ After this he made no further remarks.

31. ✘ I must have a reply without farther delay.

✔ I must have a reply without further delay.

32. ✘ Mumbai is the seaport next to Europe.

✔ Mumbai is the seaport nearest to Europe.

33. ✘ Tom's shop is nearest to the post office.

✔ Tom's shop is next to the post office.

34. ✘ My aunt lives in the nearest house.

✔ My aunt lives in the next house.

35. ✘ Both the tiger and the leopard are cats; the former animal is much larger than the later.

✔ Both the tiger and the leopard are cats: the former animal is much larger than the latter.

36. ✘ The utter meaning of this letter is not clear.

✔ The inner meaning of this letter is not clear.

37. ✘ My older brother is a doctor.

✔ My elder brother is a doctor.

38. ✘ This man is an outer fool.

✔ This man is an utter fool.

39. ✘ The ulterior wall of this house is made of stone.

✔ The exterior wall of this house is made of stone.

40. ✘ I have no exterior motive in offering you help.

✔ I have no ulterior motive in offering you help.

41. ✘ His age is of a miner importance.

✔ His age is of a minor importance.

42. ✘ Tom is inferior than John in intelligence.

✔ Tom is inferior to John in intelligence.

43. ✘ John's intelligence is superior than Tom's.

✔ John's intelligence is superior to Tom's.

44. ✘ The death of king Edward was prior than the Great War.

✔ The death of king Edward was prior to the Great War.

45. ✘ He is junior than all his colleagues.

✔ He is Junior to all his colleagues.

46. ✘ All his colleagues are senior than him.

✔ All his colleagues are senior to him.

47. ✘ The Times is the more powerful newspaper in England.

✔ The Times is the most powerful newspaper in England.

48. ✘ In India, no other exercise is so healthier as swimming.

✔ In India, no other exercise is so healthy as swimming.

49. ✘ Shakespeare is greatest than any other English poet.

✔ Shakespeare is greater than any other English poet.

50. ✗ Samudra Gupta was one of the greater of Indian kings.

✔ Samudra Gupta was one of the greatest of Indian kings.

51. ✗ Lead is heavier than all other metals.

✔ Lead is heavier than any other metal.

52. ✗ The tiger is the more ferocious of all animals.

✔ The tiger is the most ferocious of all animals.

53. ✗ Some people have much money than brains.

✔ Some people have more money than brains.

54. ✗ A wiser enemy is better than a foolish friend.

✔ A wise enemy is better than a foolish friend.

55. ✗ The Marwaries are not less enterprising than all other communities in India.

✔ The Marwaries are not less enterprising than any other community in India.

56. ✗ You do not know him well than I do.

✔ You do not know him better than I do.

57. ✗ No man was as strong as Bhim.

✔ No other man was as strong as Bhim.

58. ✗ Many Pathans were at least as faithful as the Sikhs.

✔ Some Pathans were at least as faithful as the Sikhs.

59. ✗ Mount Everest is the higher peak of the Himalayas.

✔ Mount Everest is the highest peak of the Himalayas.

60. ✗ It is easy to preach than to practise.

✔ It is easier to preach than to practise.

61. ✗ Sir Surendranath was at least as great an orator as other Indian.

✔ Sir Surendranath was at least as great an orator as any other Indian.

62. ✗ Ooty is not more healthy as any hill-station in India.

✔ Ooty is as healthy as any hill-station in India.

63. ✗ The pen is mighty than the sword.

✔ The pen is mightier than the sword.

64. ✗ He is a public notary.

✔ He is a notary public.

65. ✗ You are the apparent heir of the property.

✔ You are the heir apparent of the property.

66. ✗ The Ganges has been flowing since immemorial time.

✔ The Ganges has been flowing since time immemorial.

67. ✗ The elect viceroy has entered the hall.

✔ The viceroy elect has entered the hall.

68. ✗ I shall buy any mangoes.

✔ I shall buy some mangoes.

69. ✗ I shall not buy some mangoes.

✔ I shall not buy any mangoes.

70. ✗ Has he bought some mangoes?

✔ Has he bought any mangoes?

71. ✘ Will you please lend me any money?

✔ Will you please lend me some money?

72. ✘ Each seat was taken.

✔ Every seat was taken.

73. ✘ Five boys were seated on every bench.

✔ Five boys were seated on each bench.

74. ✘ Each one of these chairs is broken.

✔ Every one of these chairs is broken.

75. ✘ Leap year falls in each fourth year.

✔ Leap year falls in every fourth year.

76. ✘ She came to see me each three days.

✔ She came to see me every three days.

77. ✘ It rained each day during my stay in my village.

✔ It rained every day during may stay in my village.

78. ✘ His parents are worried as there is a little hope of his recovery.

✔ His parents are worried as there is little hope of his recovery.

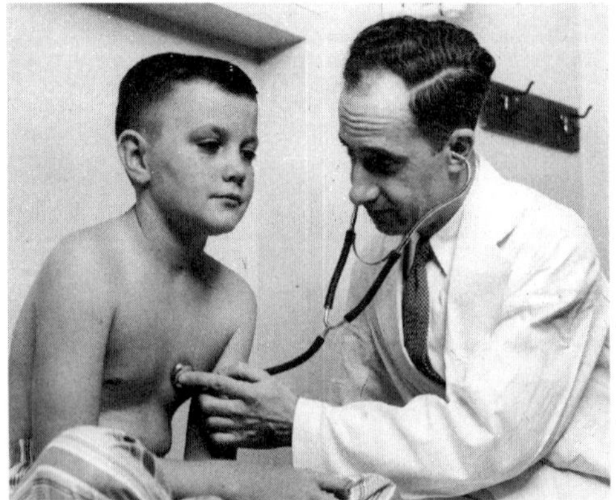

79. ✘ Little knowledge is a dangerous thing.

✔ A little knowledge is a dangerous thing.

80. ✗ A little information I had was not quite satisfactory.

✔ The little information I had was not quite satisfactory.

81. ✗ A few persons can keep a secret.

✔ Few persons can keep a secret.

82. ✗ Few words spoken in earnest will convince him.

✔ A few words spoken in earnest will convince him.

83. ✗ A few remarks that he made were very suggestive.

✔ The few remarks he made were very suggestive.

CLUES

1. The positive degree of an adjective is the adjective in its simple form and it is used when no comparision is made; as,

   She is a strong girl.

2. The Comparative Degree of an Adjective denotes a higher degree of the quality than the positive and is used when two things are compared; as

   This girl is stronger than that.

3. The Superlative Degree of an Adjective denotes the highest degree of quality and is used when more than two things are compared; as,

   This girl is the strongest in the class.

4. 'Later' and 'latest' refer to time.
5. 'Latter and 'last' refer to position.
6. 'Elder and 'eldest' are used only of persons, not of animals or things, and are confined to members of the same family.
7. 'Elder' is not used with 'than' following.
8. 'Older' and 'Oldest are used of both persons and things.

9. 'Farther means more distant or advanced.
10. 'Further' means additional.
11. 'Nearest' denotes distance.
12. 'Next denotes position.
13. The Comparative Degree is generally followed by 'than' but Comparative Adjectives ending in - 'or' are followed by the preposition 'to': as

    Inferior, superior, prior, anterior, posterior, senior, junior.
14. 'Some' is used in affirmative sentences to express quantity or degree.
15. 'Any' is used in negative and interrogative sentences.
16. 'Some' is correctly used in questions which are really commands or requests; as, will you please lend me some money?
17. 'Each and 'every' are similar in meaning but 'every' is a stronger word than 'each'.

    It means each without exception.

    'Each' is used in speaking of two or more things. 'Every' is used only in speaking of 'more than two'.

    'Each' directs attention to the individuals forming any group.

    'Every' directs attention to the total group.

    'Each' is used only when the number in the group is limited and definite.

    'Every' is used when the number is indefinite.
18. The adjective 'little has a negative meaning; as,

    There is little hope of his recovery - i.e., he is not likely to recover.
19. 'A little' has a positive meaning, as, there is a little hope of his recovery i.e., - he may possibly recover.
20. 'The little' means — not much, but all there is, as,

The little information he had was not dependable.

21. 'Few' has a negative meaning as,

    Few persons can keep a secret.

22. 'A few' has a positive meaning; as,

    A few words spoken in earnest will convince him.

23. 'The few' means — not many but all there are; as,

The few remarks he made were very suggestive. The sentence means — The remarks he made were not many but all those remarks were very suggestive.

4

Pitfalls in the Use of Adverb

An adverb is a word which modifies the meaning of a verb, an adjective or another adverb. Sometimes adverbs confuse us because we fail to distinguish them from adjectives. Sometimes, it is not easy to use adverbs correctly and so they go awry making our sentences incorrect. Carefully study the following sentences and the correct use of Adverb :

1. ✘ Ice melts fastly in the sun.
   ✔ Ice melts fast in the sun.
2. ✘ The movie was mostly over when we entered the hall.
   ✔ The movie was almost over when we entered the hall.
3. ✘ I slept good last night.
   ✔ I slept well last night.
4. ✘ He succeeded because he worked hardly.
   ✔ He succeeded because he worked hard.
5. ✘ He is looking quite good and healthy.
   ✔ He is looking quite well and healthy.

6. ✗ Are you feeling good now?
   ✓ Are you feeling better now?
7. ✗ They treated us fair.
   ✓ They treated us fairly.
8. ✗ He kicked the football highly over the spectators' head.
   ✓ He kicked the football high over the spectators' head.
9. ✗ We can't hardly believe what you say.
   ✓ We can hardly believe what you say.
10. ✗ These mangoes taste sourly.
    ✓ These mangoes taste sour.

11. ✗ You sing good.
    ✓ You sing well.
12. ✗ The cop hit the thief hardly on the shoulder.
    ✓ The cop hit the thief hard on the shoulder.
13. ✗ Don't treat him rough.
    ✓ Don't treat him roughly.
14. ✗ You should not read fastly.
    ✓ You should not read fast.
15. ✗ She was all dressed in white.
    ✓ She was dressed all in white.
16. ✗ Drive the nail straightly.
    ✓ Drive the nail straight.
17. ✗ He will sure appreciate your work.
    ✓ He will surely appreciate your work.
18. ✗ Johnson quickly runs.
    ✓ Johnson runs quickly.
19. ✗ She was sitting closely beside him.
    ✓ She was sitting close beside him.

20. ✘ At what hour right is the sun above us?
    ✔ At what hour is the sun right above us?

21. ✘ You are mistaken probably.
    ✔ Probably you are mistaken.

22. ✘ The figures are incorrect evidently.
    ✔ Evidently the figures are incorrect.

23. ✘ No one was present there unfortunately.
    ✔ Unfortunately no one was present there.

24. ✘ He escaped unhurt luckily.
    ✔ Luckily he escaped unhurt.

25. ✘ We shall begin now to work.
    ✔ We shall now begin to work.

26. ✘ That day she late arrived.
    ✔ That day she arrived late.

27. ✘ I have before heard this.
    ✔ I have heard this before.

28. ✘ Wasted time returns never.
    ✔ Wasted time never returns.

29. ✘ We have twice told you.
    ✔ We have told you twice.

30. ✘ He makes mistakes often.
    ✔ He often makes mistakes.

31. ✘ She tries to do her best always.
    ✔ She always tries to do her best.

32. ✘ He comes here seldom.
    ✔ He seldom comes here.

33. ✘ This book is written well.
    ✔ This book is well written.

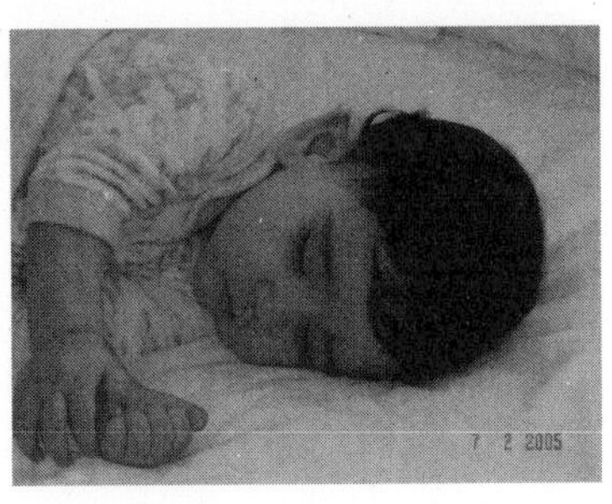

34. ✗ You clearly read.
    ✓ You read clearly.
35. ✗ The baby soundly slept.
    ✓ The baby slept soundly.
36. ✗ She is prepared fully.
    ✓ She is fully prepared.

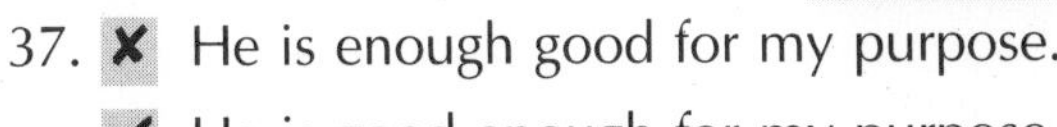

37. ✗ He is enough good for my purpose.
    ✓ He is good enough for my purpose.

38. ✗ You are mistaken altogether.
    ✓ You are altogether mistaken.

39. ✗ How bright the moon shines!
    ✓ How brightly the moon shines!
40. ✗ John can bowl fastly.
    ✓ John can bowl fast.
41. ✗ I can afford ill to lose him.
    ✓ I can ill afford to lose him.
42. ✗ Don't talk so loudly.
    ✓ Don't talk so loud.

43. ✗ She sings enough well.
    ✓ She sings well enough.
44. ✗ The patient is better much.
    ✓ The patient is much better.
45. ✗ She works hardly.
    ✓ She works hard.
46. ✗ I could hard recognize him.
    ✓ I could hardly recognize him.
47. ✗ John and Harry are related nearly.
    ✓ John and Harry are nearly related.

48. ✘ We have not recently seen him.
✔ We have not seen him recently.

49. ✘ You are sure pretty of the reality.
✔ You are pretty sure of the reality.

50. ✘ The more the merry.
✔ The more the merrier.

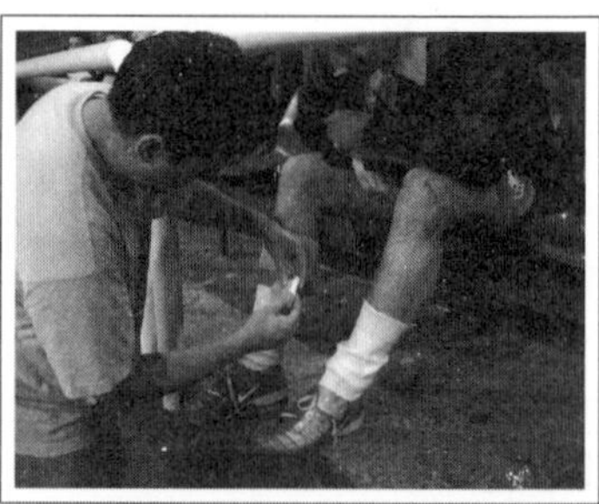

51. ✘ The fewer the good.
✔ The fewer the better.

52. ✘ The wound is deep skin.
✔ The wound is skin deep.

53. ✘ She speaks well English.
✔ She speaks English well.

54. ✘ It is heavily raining.
✔ It is raining heavily.

55. ✘ I yesterday met him.
✔ I met him yesterday.

56. ✘ He has gone out just.
✔ He has just gone out.

57. ✘ I have told you often to write neatly.
✔ I have often told you the write neatly.

58. ✘ He has seen a tiger never.
✔ He has never seen a tiger.

59. ✘ I agree with you quite.
✔ I quite agree with you.

60. ✘ He is late for school never.
✔ He is never late for school.

61. ✘ He is at home always on Sundays.
✔ He is always at home on Sundays.

62. ✗ He has often to go to college on foot.
    ✓ He often has to go to college on foot.

63. ✗ He used to always agree with me.
    ✓ He always used to agree with me.

64. ✗ Is the box enough big?
    ✓ Is the box big enough?

65. ✗ You were enough rash to interrupt.
    ✓ You were rash enough to interrupt.

66. ✗ She spoke enough loud to be heard.
    ✓ She spoke loud enough to be heard.

CLUES

1. Adverbs of manner which answer the question 'How'? (e.g., *well, last, quickly, carefully etc.*) are generally placed after the verb or after the object if there is one; as

   (i) It is raining *heavily*.

   (ii) The car is going *slowly*.

   (iii) He speaks French *well*.

2. Adverbs or Adverb phrases of place (e.g., *here, there, everywhere, on the wall*) and of time (e.g., *now, then, yet, today, next Monday*) are also usually placed after the verb or after the object, if there is one; as

   (i) She will come *here*.

   (ii) We looked *everywhere*.

   (iii) Keep the books *there*.

   (iv) She met me *yesterday*.

3. When there are two or more adverbs after a verb (and its object) the normal order is : Adverb of Manner, Adverb of Place, Adverb of Time; as,

   (i) You sang *well in the concert*

   (ii) I should go *there tomorrow evening*.

(iii) The minister spoke *earnestly at the meeting last night.*

4. Adverbs of frequency which answer the question 'How often?' (e.g., *always, never, often, rarely, usually, generally*) and certain other adverbs like *almost, already, hardly, nearly, just, quite,* are normally put between the subject and the verb if the verb consists of only one word; if there is more than one word in the verb, they are put after the first verb; as,

   (i) She *never* cooks.

   (ii) I have *never* seen a tiger.

   (iii) She has *often* told me to write neatly.

   (iv) We *usually* have breakfast at seven.

   (v) My father has *just* gone out.

   (vi) I *quite* agree with you.

5. If the verb is am\are\is\was, these adverbs are placed after the verb; as,

   (i) He is *never* late for school.

   (ii) I am *always* at home on Sundays.

   (iii) We are *just* off.

6. These adverbs are usually put before an auxiliary or the single verb *be,* when it is stressed; as,

   (i) "John has come late again" "yes, he *always* does come late".

   (ii) "When will you write the letter?" "But I *already* have written it.

   (iii) "Will you be free on Sundays?" "I *usually* am free on Sundays."

   (iv) "Do you eat meat?" "Yes, I *sometimes* do."

   When an auxiliary is used alone in short responses, as is the last examples above, it is stressed and therefore the adverb comes before it.

7. The auxiliaries *have to* and *used to* prefer the adverb in front of them; as,

   (i) We *often* have to go to school on foot.

   (ii) She always used to agree with me.

8. When an adverb modifies an adjective or another adverb, the adverb usually comes before it; as,

   (i) Darcy is *often* a lazy girl.

   (ii) The cat was *quite* dead.

   (iii) The story is very *interesting*.

   (iv) Do not walk *so* fast.

9. The adverb *enough* is always placed after the word which it modifies; as

   (i) Is the almirah big *enough* ?

   (ii) She was rash *enough* to drive.

   (iii) The speaker spoke loud *enough* to be heard.

10. As a general rule, the word *only* should be placed before the word it modifies; as,

   (i) He worked *only* three sums

   (ii) I have slept *only* two hours.

11. In spoken English, however, it is only put before the verb. The required meaning is obtained by stressing the word which the *only* modifies; as,

   (i) He *only* worked three sums.

   (ii) I have *only* slept two hours.

5

Omissions In Punctuation

Punctuation marks are stops and pauses used in writing. An incorrect and perfunctory use of these points can change the sense of a sentence completely. Punctuation involves use of standardized marks in printing and writing to separate sentences or sentence elements to make meaning clear and intelligible to the reader who in turn can have an access to the writer's exact thinking as quickly as possible with the help of these pauses called punctuation marks.

1. ✘ Ram John Darcy and their parents were present.

   ✔ Ram, John, Darcy and their parents were present.

2. ✘ He was deserted by friends relations parents and spouse.

   ✔ He was deserted by friends, relations, parents and spouse.

3. ✘ The path was tiresome tortuous and dull.

   ✔ The path was tiresome, tortuous and dull.

4. ✘ One should be sincere and honest punctual and dutiful.

   ✔ One should be sincere and honest, punctual and dutiful.

5. ✘ It being very hot we decided not to go out.

   ✔ It being very hot, we decided not to go out.

6. ✘ The weather being fine we decided to sail.

   ✔ The weather being fine, we decided to sail.

7. ✘ Rama the king of Ayodhaya, was sent on exile.

   ✔ Rama, the king of Ayodhaya, was sent on exile.

8. ✘ Shakespeare the great English playwright lived in seventeenth century.

   ✔ Shakespeare, the great English playwright, lived in seventeenth century.

9. ✘ Help me in my crisis Krishna.

   ✔ Help me in my crisis, Krishna.

10. ✘ India the country of many cultures I love thee.

    ✔ India, the country of many cultures, I love thee.

11. ✘ Slowly at last they won the victory.

    ✔ Slowly, at last, they won the victory.

12. ✘ Your story in many ways is flawed.

    ✔ Your story, in many ways, is flawed.

13. ✘ They could not however win the race.

    ✔ They could not, however, win the race.

14. ✘ You should not I repeat have any quarrel with me.

    ✔ You should not, I repeat, have any quarrel with me.

15. ✘ It is the strong determination after all that leads to success.

    ✔ It is the strong determination, after all, that leads to success.

16. ✘ You received a camera she a watch.

    ✔ You received a camera, she a watch.

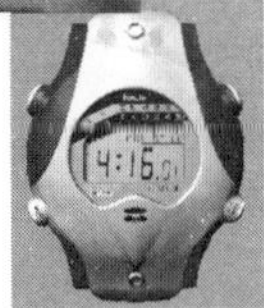

17. ✘ He is an atheist you a believer.

    ✔ He is an atheist, you a believer.

18. ✘ He came he saw he conquered.

    ✔ He came, he saw, he conquered.

19. ✘ The destination was far and we were tired.

✔ The destination was far, and we were tired.

20. ✘ He said to me "Work hard".

✔ He said to me, "Work hard".

21. ✘ To behave in such a manner is not righteousness but sin.

✔ To behave in such a manner is not righteousness, but sin.

22. ✘ All that he did to achieve success was in vain.

✔ All that he did to achieve success, was in vain.

23. ✘ How he achieved such a success is a mystery.

✔ How he achieved such a success, is a mystery.

24. ✘ That you would fail in your endeavour was not expected.

✔ That you would fail in your endeavour, was not expected.

25. ✘ Students who waste their time generally don't do well in studies.

✔ Students, who waste their time, generally don't do well in studies.

26. ✘ When she was young she played a lot of tennis.

✔ When she was young, she played a lot of tennis.

27. ✘ If you work hard you will pass.

✔ If you work hard, you will pass.

28. ✘ Rama having killed Ravana returned to Ayodhya.

✔ Rama, having killed Ravana, returned to Ayodhya.

CLUES

Comma that represents the shortest pause is used :

(i) To separate a series of words in the same construction as in sentences 1-3.

(ii) To separate each pair of words connected by 'and' as in sentence 4.

(iii) After a Nominative, Absolute as in sentences 5-6.

(iv) To mark off a Noun or Phrase in Apposition as in sentences 7-8.

(v) To mark off the Nominative of address as in sentences 9-10.

(vi) To mark off two or more adverbs or adverbial phrases coming together as in sentence 11.

(vii) Before and after words, phrases or clauses let into the body of a sentence as in sentences 12-15.

(viii) To indicate the omission of a word, especially a verb as in sentences 16-17.

(ix) To separate short coordinate clauses of a compound sentence as in sentences 18-19.

(x) To mark off a direct Quotation from the rest of the sentence as in sentence 20.

(xi) Before certain coordinating conjunctions as in sentence 21.

(xii) To separate from the verb a long subject opening a sentence as in sentence 22.

(xiii) To separate a Noun clause - whether subject or object - preceding the verb, as in sentences 22-24.

(xix) To separate a clause that is not restrictive in meaning, but is coordinate with the principal clause as in sentence 25.

(xx) To separate an Adverbial Clause from its main clause as in sentences 26-27.

(xxi) Before and after a Participle Phrase as in sentence 28.

1. ✗ He goes to office everyday

   ✓ He goes to office everyday.

2. ✗ Bring a glass of water

   ✓ Bring a glass of water.

3. ✗ His name is MS Chauhan.

   ✓ His name is M.S. Chauhan.

4. ✗ He is an MA in English.

   ✓ He is an M.A. in English.

5. ✗ You should not overlook the importance of this concept

   ✓ You should not overlook the importance of this concept.

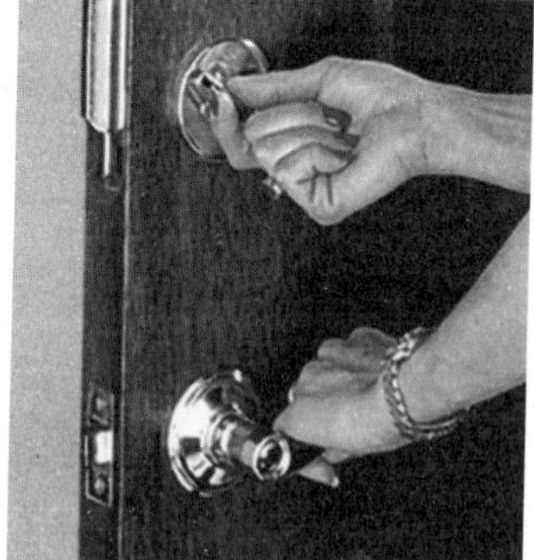

6. ✗ Please close the door

   ✓ Please close the door.

7. ✗ It is 1030 by my watch.

   ✓ It is 10.30 by my watch.

8. ✗ She has done her BA Honours in Economics.

   ✓ She has done her B.A. Honours in Economics.

CLUES

The full stop or period (.) is used.

(i) To mark the end of a Declarative or an Imperative sentence.

(ii) To mark abbreviations and initials.

1. ✘ You are courageous, bold and wise and we all admire you.

✔ You are courageous, bold and wise; and we all admire you.

2. ✘ What he was in the past he is not today what he is today he will not be tomorrow.

✔ What he was in the past; he is not today; what he is today; he will not be tomorrow.

3. ✘ He was a brave, large-hearted man and we all honoured him.

✔ He was a brave, large-hearted man; and we all honoured him.

4. ✘ Today we love what tomorrow we hate, today we seek what tomorrow we shun, today we desire what tomorrow we fear.

✔ Today we love what tomorrow we hate; today we seek what tomorrow we shun; today we desire what tomorrow we fear.

5. ✘ Her court was pure, her life serene. God gave her peace, her land reposed.

✔ Her court was pure; her life serene; God gave her peace; her land reposed.

6. ✘ John is an optimist, because he always looks at bright side of things Darcy is a pessimist, because she looks at seamy side of things.

✔ John is an optimist, because he always looks at bright side of things; Darcy is a pessimist, because she looks at seamy side of things.

7. ✘ She had three sons the eldest was married the youngest still at school.

✔ She had three sons; the eldest was married; the youngest still at school.

CLUES

(i) The semicolon represents a pause of greater importance than shown by the comma.

(ii) Semicolon is used to separate the clauses of a Compound Sentence, when they contain a comma.

(iii) Semicolon is also used to separate a series of loosely related clauses.

1. ✘ Bacon says reading makes a full man, writing an exact man, speaking a ready man.

   ✔ Bacon says : - "Reading makes a full man, writing an exact man, speaking a ready man."

2. ✘ The principal parts of verb in English are present tense, the past tense, and the past participle.

   ✔ The principal parts of verb in English are : present tense, the past tense, and the past participle.

3. ✘ The limitation of armaments, the acceptance of arbitration as the natural solvent of international disputes, the relegation of wars of ambition and aggression to the categories of obsolete follies these will be milestones which mark the stages of the road.

   ✔ The limitation of armaments, the acceptance of arbitration as the natural solvent of international disputes, the relegation of wars of ambition and aggression to the categories of absolute follies : these will be milestones which mark the stages of the road.

4. ✘ Study to acquire a habit of thinking no study is more important.

   ✔ Study to acquire a habit of thinking : no study is more important.

5. ✘ Attach the following certificate.
   ✔ Attach the following certificates:
6. ✘ Someone has rightly said "Slow and steady wins the race."
   ✔ Someone has rightly said : "Slow and steady wins the race."
7. ✘ The driver was drunk this was the cause of accident.
   ✔ The driver was drunk : this was the cause of accident.
8. ✘ My favourite authors are, William Shakespeare, John Keats and Oscar Wilde.
   ✔ My favourite authors are : William Shakespeare, John Keats and Oscar Wilde.
9. ✘ His telephone No is 26854704.
   ✔ His telephone No is : 26854704.
10. ✘ Here is another example.
   ✔ Here is another example:
11. ✘ Rewrite the following sentence.
   ✔ Rewrite the following sentence:
12. ✘ I know the commandant, he was my class-fellow.
   ✔ I know the commandant : he was my class-fellow.

CLUES

(i) The colon marks a still more complete pause than that expressed by the semicolon.

(ii) Colon is used often with a dash after it.

(iii) It is used to introduce a quotation, before enumeration, examples and before sentences grammatically independent but closely connected in sense.

1. ✘ Who teaches you English.
   ✔ Who teaches you English?

2. ✗ Do you want to come with me for a walk.
   ✔ Do you want to come with me for a walk?
3. ✗ Where do you live.
   ✔ Where do you live?
4. ✗ Have you ever been to Mussoori.
   ✔ Have you ever been to Mussoori?
5. ✗ Did you give him my message.
   ✔ Did you give him my message?

6. ✗ Could I use your telephone.
   ✔ Could I use your telephone?
7. ✗ Who is there.
   ✔ Who is there?
8. ✗ Are you going to market.
   ✔ Are you going to market?

9. ✗ Will you deliver the message in time.
   ✔ Will you deliver the message in time?
10. ✗ What would you like to have.
    ✔ What would you like to have?
11. ✗ He asked me whether I had written my exercise?
    ✔ He asked me whether I had written my exercise.
12. ✗ Do you know where he lives.
    ✔ Do you know where he lives ?
13. ✗ Did you know who had stolen the money.
    ✔ Did you know who had stolen the money?
14. ✗ I asked him where he lived?
    ✔ I asked him where he lived.

15. ✗ He came in time. Didn't he.

✔ He came in time. Didn't he?

16. ✗ I did not speak to the principal. Did I.

✔ I did not speak to the principal. Did I?

17. ✗ He speaks fluent English. Doesn't he.

✔ He speaks fluent English. Doesn't he?

18. ✗ You can't solve these sums. Can you.

✔ You can't solve these sums. Can you?

19. ✗ They did not play well. Did they.

✔ They did not play well. Did they?

20. ✗ The patient had recovered. Hadn't he.

✔ The patient had recovered. Hadn't he?

CLUES

(i) The Question Mark or Interrogation mark is used, instead of the full stop, after a direct question.

(ii) The Question Mark or Sign of Interrogation mark is not used after an Indirect Question as in sentences 11 and 14.

1. ✗ What a fine weather?

✔ What a fine weather!

2. ✗ Hurrah we have won the match.

✔ Hurrah! we have won the match.

3. ✗ Alas she is no more.

✔ Alas! she is no more.

4. ✗ May you live long?

✔ May you live long!

5. ✗ What a beautiful painting.

✔ What a beautiful painting!

6. ✗ May you be blessed with a son?

✔ May you be blessed with a son!

7. ✘ What a wonderful sight.
   ✔ What a wonderful sight!

8. ✘ How sweet the rose is?
   ✔ How sweet the rose is!

9. ✘ What a rash deed.
   ✔ What a rash deed!
10. ✘ Oh well done.
    ✔ Oh! well done.
11. ✘ Oh God I am ruined.
    ✔ Oh God! I am ruined.
12. ✘ How bravely the firemen acted.
    ✔ How bravely the firemen acted!

13. ✘ What a beautiful rainbow?
    ✔ What a beautiful rainbow!
14. ✘ What would I not give to have my childhood again?
    ✔ What would I not give to have my childhood again!
15. ✘ What a nice hit?
    ✔ What a nice hit!

16. ✗ Fie on you to be so cruel.

✔ Fie on you to be so cruel!

17. ✗ O, for a glass of cold water.

✔ O, for a glass of cold water!

18. ✗ What a terrible fire this is?

✔ What a terrible fire this is!

19. ✗ O, what a fall was there my country men?

✔ O, what a fall was there, my countrymen!

20. ✗ Long live the king.

✔ Long live the king!

21. ✗ O father I hear the sound of guns?

✔ O father! I hear the sound of guns.

22. ✗ O Hamlet, speak no more.

✔ O Hamlet, speak no more!

CLUES

(i) The sign of exclamation is used after Interjections and after Phrases and Sentences expressing sudden emotion or wish.

(ii) When the Interjection O is placed before the Nomination of Address, the Sign of Exclamation, if employed at all, comes after the noun, or it may be placed at the end of the sentence.

1. ✗ John said I am not going to office today.

✔ John said, "I am not going to office today."

2. ✗ We heard him crying Thief Thief!

✔ We heard him crying, "Thief, Thief"!

3. ✘ The student said I have done my home work.
   ✔ The student said, "I have done my home work".
4. ✘ The child said to mother I am going out.
   ✔ The child said to mother, "I am going out."
5. ✘ I met you in the party yesterday I said to him.
   ✔ "I met you in the party yesterday," I said to him.
6. ✘ My father said to me I gave you some home work yesterday.
   ✔ My father said to me, "I gave you some home work yesterday."
7. ✘ He said it may rain today.
   ✔ He said, " It may rain today."
8. ✘ She said to me will you help me.
   ✔ She said to me, "Will you help me"?
9. ✘ Do you speak good English the interviewer said to me.
   ✔ "Do you speak good English?" The interviewer said to me.
10. ✘ Has she returned your money I said to my daughter.
    ✔ "Has she returned your money"? I said to my daughter.
11. ✘ Whom did you give the money he said to me.
    ✔ "Whom did you give the money"? he said to me.
12. ✘ Where will you meet me I said to my friend.
    ✔ "Where will you meet me?" I said to my friend.
13. ✘ He said to his servant why have you disturbed me.
    ✔ He said to his servant, "Why have you disturbed me?".
14. ✘ The teacher said to the student don't make a noise.
    ✔ The teacher said to the student, "Don't make a noise".
15. ✘ He said to his servant bring a glass of water.
    ✔ He said to his servant, "Bring a glass of water."

16. ✗ I said what a horrible sight!

✔ I said, "What a horrible sight!"

17. ✗ What a bad luck he said.

✔ "What a bad luck!" he said.

18. ✗ May you live long he said to the child.

✔ "May you live long!" he said to the child.

19. ✗ I would rather die, he exclaimed than join the oppressors of my country.

✔ "I would rather die", he exclaimed, "than join the oppressors of my country."

20. ✗ Babar is said by Elphinstone to have been the most admirable prince that ever reigned in Asia.

✔ Babar is said by Elphinstone to have been "the most admirable prince that ever reigned in Asia."

21. ✗ You might as well say, added the March Hare, that I like what I get is the same thing as I get what I like.

✔ "You might as well say", added the March Hare, "that 'I like what I get' is the same thing as I get what I like."

CLUES

(i) Inverted Commas or Quotation Marks " " are used to enclose the exact words of a speaker , or a quotation.

(ii) If a quotation occurs within a quotation, it is marked by single inverted commas.

1. ✗ If I were a millionaire, but why blame the luck.

✔ If I were a millionaire — but why blame the luck?

2. ✗ Joys, sorrows sufferings all are there in human life.

✔ Joys, sorrows, sufferings — all are there in human life.

3. ✘ If my wife were alive but why lament the past?

✔ If my wife were alive — but why lament the past.

4. ✘ Friends, companions, relatives, all deserted him.

✔ Friends, companions, relatives — all deserted him.

5. ✘ At the age of four, such is the power of genius she could read and write.

✔ At the age of four such is the power of genius — she could read and write.

CLUES

(i) The Dash is used to indicate an abrupt stop or change of thought.

(ii) It is also used to resume a scattered subject.

1. ✘ You came in time it was my desire to save me.

✔ You came in time (it was my desire) to save me.

2. ✘ He gained from Heaven it was all he wished a friend.

✔ He gained from Heaven (it was all he wished) a friend.

3. ✘ At last the ordeal the hijacking of the aeroplane, one person was killed, the commandos stormed the plane came to an end.

✔ At last, the ordeal — the hijacking of the aeroplane, one person was killed, the commandos stormed the plane — came to an end.

4. ✘ A remarkable instance of this kind of courage call it if you please call it, resolute will is given in the history of Babar.

   ✔ A remarkable instance of this kind of courage — call it, if you please, resolute will — is given in the history of Babar.

CLUES

Parentheses or Double Dashes are used to separàte from the main part of the sentence, a Phrase or Clause which does not grammatically belong to it.

1. ✘ A passerby asked me if I could tell him the way to the nearest inn.

   ✔ A passer-by asked me if I could tell him the way to the nearest inn.

2. ✘ You are a jack of all trades.

   ✔ You are a jack-of-all-trades.

3. ✘ The early bird catches the worm.

   ✔ The early-bird catches the worm.

4. ✘ The state of the art equipment is installed in this office.

   ✔ The state-of-the art equipment is installed in this office.

5. ✘ An early riser can maintain his health.

   ✔ An early-riser can maintain his health.

6. ✘ I need your cooperation.

   ✔ I need your co-operation.

7. ✘ She died heart broken.

   ✔ She died heart-broken.

8. ✘ A large procession was taken out to the drum beating.

   ✔ A large procession was taken out to the drum-beating.

9. ✗ The criss cross lines were running all over her old face.

✓ The criss-cross lines were running all over her old face.

10. ✗ He seems to be a barking dog seldom bites man.

✓ He seems to be a barking-dog-seldom-bites man.

CLUES

(i) The Hyphen (-) A shorter line than Dash, is used to connect the parts of a compound word.

(ii) It is also used to connect parts of a word divided at the end of a line.

1. ✗ It is Johns book.

✓ It is Johns's book.

2. ✗ Dot your ms and cricle your ks.

✓ Dot your m's and circle your K's.

3. ✗ I dont know how to type.

✓ I don't know how to type.

4. ✗ Had you come to me Id have helped you.

✓ Had you come to me I'd have helped you.

5. ✗ Hes man of his word.

✓ He's man of his word.

6. ✗ I ve seen this movie.

✓ I've seen this movie.

7. ✗ Have you eer helped a poor man?

✓ Have you e'er helped a poor man?

8. ✗ This is fathers shirt.

✓ This is father's shirt.

9. ✘ How many 3s are there in your house number?

✔ How many 3's are there in your house number?

10. ✘ Whos done this mischief?

✔ Who's done this mischief?

11. ✘ Id reached home when the rain started.

✔ I'd reached home when the rain started.

12. ✘ Id like to have a glass of water.

✔ I'd like to have a glass of water.

13. ✘ Hes not to blame.

✔ He's not to blame.

14. ✘ You arent wrong at all.

✔ You aren't wrong at all.

15. ✘ He wont attend the party.

✔ He won't attend the party.

16. ✘ He shouldnt have done it.

✔ He shouldn't have done it.

17. ✘ I was in Singapore in 1990s.

✔ I was is Singapore in 1990's.

18. ✘ Youre totally correct.

✔ You're totally correct.

CLUES

The Apostrophe is used :

(i) To show the omission of a letter or letters.

(ii) To form the plural of letters and figures.

(iii) In the Genitive case of Noun.

1. ✘ Brazil, which is nearly as large as the whole of europe, is covered with a vegetation of incredible profusion.

✔ Brazil, which is nearly as large as the whole of Europe, is covered with a vegetation of incredible profusion.

2. ✘ In the old persian stories, turan, the land of darkness, is opposed to Iran, the land of light.

✔ In the old Persian stories, Turan, the land of darkness, is opposed to Iran, the land of light.

3. ✘ mumbai, kolkata and delhi are big cities.

✔ Mumbai, Kolkata and Delhi are big cities.

4. ✘ He is m.sc. in botany.

✔ He is M.Sc. in Botany.

5. ✘ He has specialised in french.

✔ He has specialised himself in French.

French, Bit By Bit Volume 2

6. ✘ hail to thee, blithe spirit!
bird thou never wert,
that from heaven or near it
pourest thy full heart
in profuse strains of un-premeditated art.

✔ Hail to thee, blithe spirit!
Bird thou never wert,
That from heaven or near it,
Pourest thy full heart
In profuse strains of un-premeditated art.

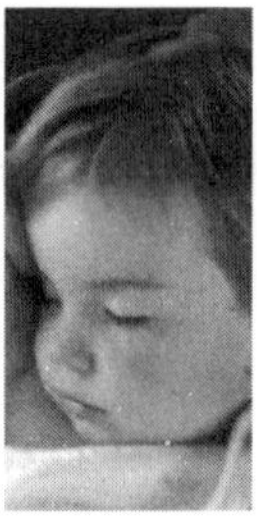

7. ✘ When I was a child, i had no worries
i was fed well and I was looked after well.

✔ When I was a child, I had no worries,
I was fed well and I was looked after well.

8. ✘ i would like to apply to the grant of a district board scholarship, to enable me to continue my studies in a university college.

✔ I would like to apply for the grant of a District Board Scholarship to enable me to continue my studies in a University College.

9. ✗ Amongst the courtiers sat count de lorge beside a beautiful and lively lady of noble birth.

✓ Amongst the courtiers sat Count de Lorge beside a beautiful and lively lady of noble birth.

10. ✗ king francis was a great lover of all kinds of sport; and one day he and his courtiers, noblemen and ladies, sat watching wild savage lions fighting each other in the enclosure below.

✓ King Francis was a great lover of all kinds of sport; and one day he and his courtiers, noblemen and ladies, sat watching wild savage lions fighting each other in the enclosure below.

CLUES

Capital letters are used :-

(i) To begin a sentence.

(ii) To begin each fresh line of poetry.

(iii) To begin all Proper Nouns and Adjectives derived from them.

(iv) For all Nouns and Pronouns which indicate the Deity.

(v) To write the pronoun 'I' and Interjection O.

6

Negligences in Direct and Indirect Speech

Many lapses are seen in direct and indirect narration. They can be easily avoided if the rules of narration are followed strictly.

When the Reporting Verb is in the Past Tense, all clauses of the Direct Narration in the Present Tense, are changed into corresponding past Tenses in Indirect speech.

If the reporting verb is in the Present or Future Tense, the clauses of Direct Narration do not change into corresponding Past Tenses in Indirect Speech.

When the Direct Narration expresses some universal truth, the tense of the Reported Speech does not change.

The words of Reported Speech expressing nearness in time or place are changed into those of distance. Modals — shall, will, can, may and other auxilaries — do, does, is, are am etc are changed into Past Tense.

If there is an object after the Reporting Verb, then 'said' is changed into 'told'.

Pronouns and Possessives are also changed according to the sense of the sentence.

While reporting questions, (interrogative sentences) Indirect Speech is introduced by such verbs as 'asked', 'inquired' in place of 'said or told'.

In reporting Imperative Sentences, the Reporting Narration is introduced by some such verbs as express command or request.

In reporting Exclamatory Sentences, expressions such as — 'exclaimed with joy' or 'exclaimed with sorrow' are used.

In Indirect Narration the inverted commas " " are removed.

In Indirect speech, all sentences become Assertive.

1. ✘ He said to me that he has given me much trouble.
   ✔ He told me that he had given me much trouble.
2. ✘ The student told the teacher that he has done his work.
   ✔ The student told the teacher that he had done his work.
3. ✘ The teacher told the students that she is giving them a small home work.
   ✔ The teacher told the students that she was giving them a small home work.
4. ✘ She told me that she will meet me tomorrow.
   ✔ She told me that she would meet me the next day.
5. ✘ The boys told that they have completed the work.
   ✔ The boys said that they had completed the work.
6. ✘ The child said to his mother that he was going out.
   ✔ The child told his mother that he was going out.
7. ✘ I told him that I met him in the party yesterday.
   ✔ I told him that I had met him in the party the previous day.
8. ✘ My father told me that he gave me some home work the previous day.
   ✔ My father told me that he had given me some home work the previous day.

9. ✘ He said to me that he took exercise everyday.

✔ He told me that he took exercise everyday.

10. ✘ The boys told that they took part in the cultural programmes of their school.

✔ The boys said that they took part in the cultural programmes of their school.

11. ✘ He told us that we have not taken serious interest in our studies.

✔ He told us that we had not taken serious interest in our studies.

12. ✘ The students said that they have been studying in this school for five years.

✔ The students said that they had been studying in that school for five years.

13. ✘ The principal announced that the examinations are likely to be postponed for a fortnight.

✔ The principal announced that the examinations were likely to be postponed for a fortnight.

14. ✘ The teacher said to the students that they have been learning English for six months but they have not improved the language yet.

✔ The teacher told the students that they had been learning English for six months but they had not improved the language yet.

15. ✘ He told me that he went to my home yesterday.

✔ He told me that he had gone to my home the previous day.

16. ✘ The principal told the students that only those students who are hardworking, sincere and disciplined, bring a good name to their parents and country.

✔ The principal told the students that only those students who were hardworking, sincere and disciplined, brought good name to their parents and country.

17. ✘ He said to the people that he shot the tiger with his gun.

✔ He told the people that he had shot the tiger with his gun.

18. ✘ The publisher said that this newspaper appears twice a week.

✔ The publisher said that that newspaper appeared twice a week.

19. ✘ You told me that you have had your food.

✔ You told me that you had had your food.

20. ✘ I said to my father that I wish to join computer classes after I pass my senior secondary examination.

✔ I told my father that I wished to join computer classes after I passed my senior secondary examination.

CLUES

(i) If the reporting verb is in the past tense the reported speech, in one sentence or different clauses changes into past Tense; as,

He said to me, "I am tired".

He said to me — is Reporting Verb.

"I am tired" — is Reported Speech.

He told me that he was tired.

(ii) Said to - changes to 'told'

(iii) No preposition (to) is used after 'told'

(iv) If the speaker in the Reporting verb is not speaking to a particular person, 'told' is not used; as,

They said, "we go for a walk".

They said that they went for a walk.

(v) Present Simple Tense in Direct Speech changes into Past Simple in Indirect Speech.

(vi) Present Continuous Tense in Direct Speech changes into Past Continuous Tense in Indirect Speech.

(vii) Present Perfect Tense in Direct Speech changes into Past Perfect Tense in Indirect Speech.

(viii) Present Perfect Continuous Tense in Direct Speech changes into Past Perfect Continuous Tense in Indirect Speech.

(ix) Past Simple Tense in Direct Speech also changes into Past Perfect Tense in Indirect Speech.

(x) Past Continuous Tense in Direct Speech also changes into Past Perfect Continuous Tense in Indirect Speech.

(xi) 'This' in Direct Speech changes into 'that' in Indirect Speech.

(xii) 'Tomorrow' in Direct Speech changes into 'the next day' or 'the day after', in Indirect Speech.

(xiii) 'Yesterday' in Direct Speech changes into 'the previous day' or 'the day before', in Indirect Speech.

21. ✘ I said to him if he took this route to his office.

✔ I asked him if he took that route to his office.

22. ✘ My father asked me if had I met my friend?

✔ My father asked me if I had met my friend.

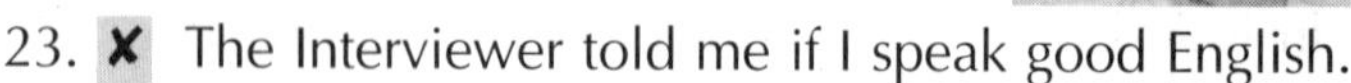

23. ✘ The Interviewer told me if I speak good English.

✔ The interviewer asked me if I spoke good English.

24. ✘ I told my servant if he has any thing new to say.

✔ I asked my servant if he had any thing new to say.

25. ✘ You asked me if she will attend the party.

✔ You asked me if she would attend the party.

26. ✘ I asked my sister if she met her friend in the party last night?

✔ I asked my sister if she had met her friend in the party the night before.

27. ✘ The teacher told the students if they had done their class work?

✔ The teacher asked the students if they had done their class work.

28. ✘ I asked my daughter if he has returned her money.

✔ I asked my daughter if he had returned her money.

29. ✘ He asked me whether if I would guide him to the nearest bus stop.

✔ He asked me whether I would guide him to the nearest bus stop.

30. ✘ He asked me if I am going to market.

✔ He asked me if I was going to market.

31. ✘ He asked me that if I had done my work.

✔ He asked me if I had done my work.

CLUES

(i) All Interrogative Sentences become Assertive sentences when they are changed into Indirect Speech.

(ii) No interrogation mark (?) is used when an interrrogative sentence has been changed into Indirect Speech.

(iii) As all Interrogative Sentences become Assertive sentences in Indirect speech, Noun or Pronoun is used before the verb.

(iv) Reporting verbs 'said to' and 'told' are not used when interrogative sentences are changed into Indirect Speech.

(v) Verbs - 'asked' or 'inquired' are used when Interrogative Sentences are changed into Indirect Speech.

32. ✘ He asked me whether where I kept my books.

    ✔ He asked me where I kept my books.

33. ✘ I asked him that how he went to office.

    ✔ I asked him how he went to office.

34. ✘ I asked my friend if who taught him English.

    ✔ I asked my friend who taught him English.

35. ✘ I asked him that what he was doing?

    ✔ I asked him what he was doing.

36. ✘ I asked him when will the next mail come.

    ✔ I asked him when the next mail would come.

37. ✘ He inquired whether the school will remain closed the next day.

    ✔ He inquired whether the school would remain closed the next day.

38. ✘ My friend asked me whether where I kept my books.

    ✔ My friend asked me where I kept my books.

39. ✘ My father asked me if who taught me English?

    ✔ My father asked me who taught me English.

40. ✘ My employer asked me when I will come back from the tour.

    ✔ My employer asked me when I would come back from the tour.

CLUES

(i) While changing Interrogative sentences with Interrogative words (who, whom, why, what, where, which, when, how) into Indirect Speech, conjunctions 'whether' or 'if' are not used but the same interrogative word — who, whom, what , where, which, when, how — is used in Indirect speech.

(ii) 'Will' changes to 'would' in Indirect speech.

(iii) 'Shall' also changes to 'would' in indirect speech.

Note : 'Shall' changes to 'should' only when it is used for permission; as,

He said, "Shall I go?"
He asked if he should go.

(iv) Either 'if' or 'whether' is used in Indirect Speech. Both the conjunctions cannot be used together.

(v) Conjunctions 'if' or 'whether' and the interrogative word cannot be used together.

(vi) 'That' and 'told' are never used when Interrogative Sentences, whether beginning with Auxiliaries or with Interrogative Words are changed into Indirect Speech.

41. ✘ He said that he can solve that sum.

✔ He said that he could solve that sum.

42. ✘ The students told the teacher that it may not be possible for them to solve all the sums.

✔ The students told the teacher that it might not be possible for them to solve all the sums.

43. ✘ He asked a passerby if he (the passerby) can tell him the way to the nearest inn.

✔ He asked a passerby if he (the passerby) could tell him the way to the nearest inn.

44. ✗ I asked my mother if I may go out to play.

✔ I asked my mother if I might go out to play.

45. ✗ The Meteorological Deptt predicted that it may rain tomorrow.

✔ The Meteorological Deptt predicted that it might rain the next day.

CLUES

Modals — 'can' becomes 'could' and 'may' becomes 'might' in Indirect Speech.

46. ✗ The teacher said that honesty was the best policy.

✔ The teacher said that honesty is the best policy.

47. ✗ He said that the sun rose in the east.

✔ He said that the sun rises in the east.

48. ✗ He said that two and two made four.

✔ He said that two and two make four.

CLUES

When the Direct Narration expresses some universal truth, the tense of the reported speech does not change.

49. ✗ He says that he would help the needy.

✔ He says that he will help the needy.

50. ✗ He will say that he would come in time.

✔ He will say that he will come in time.

51. ✗ He says that he was ten years of age.

✔ He says that he is ten years of age.

CLUES

If the Reporting verb is in the Present Tense or Future Tense, the tense of the Reported Speech in one clause or more clauses does not change.

52. ✗ I asked him what did he want.

✔ I asked him what he wanted.

53. ✘ The interviewer asked me what is my father's name.

✔ The interviewer asked me what my father's name was.

54. ✘ She asked me who there was.

✔ She asked me who was there.

55. ✘ I know where were you.

✔ I know where you were.

56. ✘ She told me that she knows who taught me English.

✔ She told me that she knew who taught me English.

57. ✘ She asked me who teaches me English.

✔ She asked me who taught me English.

CLUES

(i) In sentence No. 52 'did' can't be used in Indirect speech because when an Interrogative Sentence of Present Simple Tense introduced with auxiliary 'Do' in Direct speech, is changed into Indirect speech, it will take 'past' form of the main verb 'want' and did can't be used because the sentence in Indirect Speech is no more an Interrogative Sentence but an Assertive Sentence.

(ii) In sentence No. 53 the possessive 'my father's shall come before the verb 'was' as all interrogative sentences' become 'Assertive Sentences' when they are changed into Indirect Speech.

(iii) In sentence No. 54 the first construction is wrong because 'who' is doing the function of a relative pronoun and there is no other noun or pronoun to be placed before the verb 'was'.

(iv) In sentence 55 pronoun 'you' should come before the verb 'were'.

(v) In sentence No.56 the Subordinate Clause should be placed in Past Tense because the Main Clause of the Reporting verb is in the Past Tense.

58. ✘ He said to his servant to bring a glass of water.
    ✔ He ordered his servant to bring a glass of water.

59. ✘ He requested me to please close the door.
    ✔ He requested me to close the door.

60. ✘ The commander commanded the soldiers to please move forward.
    ✔ The commander commanded the soldiers to move forward.

61. ✘ The teacher ordered the students to don't make a noise.
    ✔ The teacher ordered the students not to make a noise.

62. ✘ I advised him to not to drive fast.
    ✔ I advised him not to drive fast.

63. ✘ The mother told the son to make haste.
    ✔ The mother asked the son to make haste.

64. ✘ He ordered the guests to please not to park your cars here.
    ✔ He requested the guests not to park their cars there.

65. ✘ He ordered the children to not to make a noise.
    ✔ He ordered the children not to make a noise.

66. ✘ The gardener said to the children to don't pluck flowers.

✔ The gardener ordered the children not to pluck flowers.

CLUES

(i) When changing Imperative Sentences into Indirect Speech, verbs such as ordered / requested / asked / advised / commanded / threatened etc are used according to the sense of the sentences.

(ii) Infinitive 'to' is used followed by the Present Form of the verb.

(iii) 'not to' + present from of the verb is used in Negative Commands.

(iv) Word 'please' should not form part of the sentences if the verb 'Requested' has been used.

(v) Verb 'told' should not be used while changing Imperative sentences into Indirect Speech.

(vi) Verb 'asked' can be used while changing Interrogative sentences as well as Imperative Sentences into Indirect Speech.

67. ✘ They said that what a fine weather!

✔ They exclaimed with joy that it was a very fine weather.

68. ✘ The boys said hurrah we have won the match.

✔ The boys exclaimed joyfully that they had won the match.

69. ✘ The spectators exclaimed that what a fine hit.

✔ The spectators exclaimed joyfully that it was very fine hit.

70. ✘ They exclaimed sorrowfully that Alas her only son is dead.

✔ They exclaimed sorrowfully that her only son was dead.

71. ✘ He said what a terrible rain!

✔ He exclaimed that it was a terrible rain.

72. ✗ He exclaimed sorrowfully what a bad luck.

✔ He exclaimed sorrowfully that it was a bad luck.

73. ✗ He said to the child may you live long!

✔ He prayed to God that the child might live long.

CLUES

(i) While changing Exclamatory sentences and Optative (wish) sentences into Indirect Speech, expressions such as — exclaimed with joy or exclaimed joyfully, 'exclaimed with sorrow' or 'exclaimed sorrowfully' are used.

(ii) Conjunction 'that' is used to join the sentence.

(iii) The tense changes into Past Tense as done in the case of an Assertive Sentence.

(iv) Exclamatory mark is removed in Indirect Speech.

(v) An exclamatory sentence is changed into a complete Assertive sentence with exclamatory connotations in Indirect speech.

74. ✗ He said to me I am tired.

✔ He said to me, "I am tired."

75. ✗ He said I cannot work.

✔ He said, "I cannot work."

76. ✗ I shall meet you tomorrow she said to me.

✔ "I shall meet you tomorrow", she said to me.

77. ✗ Will she attend the party you asked me.

✔ "Will she attend the party?", you asked me.

78. ✘ The boys said we have completed the work.

✔ The boys said, "We have completed the work."

79. ✘ I said to him do you take this route to your office.

✔ I said to him, "Do you take this route to your office?"

80. ✘ I asked my friend who teaches you English.

✔ I asked my friend, "Who teaches you English?"

CLUES

(i) When we repeat the actual words of a speaker, we use Direct Speech.

(ii) In Direct speech, we use Inverted Commas " " to use the exact words spoken by the speaker.

(iii) The first letter of the first word to be kept within Inverted Commas " " is always capital.

7

Errors in the Use of Articles

Study the following sentences carefully to learn the correct use of articles :

1. ✘ The copper is an useful metal.
   ✔ Copper is a useful metal.
2. ✘ She is not a honourable woman.
   ✔ She is not an honourable woman.
3. ✘ The Haridwar is a holy city.
   ✔ Haridwar is a holy city.
4. ✘ The ableman has not always a distinguished look.
   ✔ An ableman has not always a distinguished look.
5. ✘ The honest men speak the truth.
   ✔ Honest men speak the truth.
6. ✘ Do you see a blue sky?
   ✔ Do you see the blue sky?
7. ✘ Aladdin had the wonderful lamp.
   ✔ Aladdin had a wonderful lamp.
8. ✘ He returned after a hour.
   ✔ He returned after an hour.

9. ✗ School will shortly close for Puja holidays.
   ✔ The school will shortly close for the Puja holidays.

10. ✗ A sun shines brightly.
    ✔ The sun shines brightly.
11. ✗ An European called at my office.
    ✔ A European called at my office.
12. ✗ The Sanskrit is a difficult language.
    ✔ Sanskrit is a difficult language.
13. ✗ Ganga is a sacred river.
    ✔ The Ganga is a sacred river.

14. ✗ A lion is a king of beasts.
    ✔ The lion is the king of beasts.
15. ✗ French is a easy language.
    ✔ French is an easy language.

16. ✗ French defeated the Germans.
    ✔ The French defeated the Germans.
17. ✗ Which is a longest river in India?
    ✔ Which is the longest river is India?
18. ✗ They found a egg in nest.
    ✔ They found an egg in the nest.
19. ✗ He bought a horse, a ox and a buffalo.
    ✔ He bought a horse, an ox and a buffalo.

20. ✗ The guide knows a way.
    ✔ The guide knows the way.
21. ✗ English is a language of the people of England.
    ✔ English is the language of the people of England.

22. ✗ You are a untidy girl.

✔ You are an untidy girl.

23. ✗ Ceylon is the island.

✔ Ceylon is an island.

24. ✗ Let us discuss a matter seriously.

✔ Let us discuss the matter seriously.

25. ✗ She got a first prize.

✔ She got the first prize.

26. ✗ You are a honour to your profession.

✔ You are an honour to your profession.

27. ✗ He looks as stupid as the owl.

✔ He looks as stupid as an owl.

28. ✗ This is a longest bridge in India.

✔ This is the longest bridge in India.

29. ✗ They sailed to south.

✔ They sailed to the south.

30. ✗ You have come without the umbrella.

✔ You have come without an umbrella.

31. ✗ Gold is an useful metal.

✔ Gold is a useful metal.

32. ✗ She waited for me for a hour.

✔ She waited for me for an hour.

33. ✗ I saw an one-eyed man.

✔ I saw a one-eyed man.

34. ✗ She is an university professor.

✔ She is a university professor.

35. ✗ A book you presented me has been lost.

✓ The book you presented me has been lost.

36. ✗ How beautiful a sky looks!

✓ How beautiful the sky looks.

37. ✗ Sun sets in west.

✓ The sun sets in the west.

38. ✗ Has he been told about accident?

✓ Has he been told about the accident?

39. ✗ He has not seen me since I was infant.

✓ He has not seen me since I was an infant.

40. ✗ We saw queer object floating in sky.

✓ We saw a queer object floating in the sky.

41. ✗ The boys played cricket in park.

✓ The boys played cricket in the park.

42. ✗ I have solved all questions.

✓ I have solved all the questions.

43. ✗ I learned French from aged Jew.

✓ I learned French from an aged Jew.

44. ✗ Qutab Minar is famous historical monument.

✓ Qutab Minar is a famous historical monument.

45. ✗ London is on Thames.

✓ London is on the Thames.

46. ✗ You have scored best marks.

✔ You have scored the best marks.

47. ✘ This is one of best books written by Shakespeare.

✔ This is one of the best books written by Shakespeare.

48. ✘ Where did you buy present?

✔ Where did you buy the present?

49. ✘ Her knowledge of medicine had been acquired under aged Jewers.

✔ Her knowledge of the medicine had been acquired under an aged Jewers.

50. ✘ The brave soldier lost arm in battle.

✔ The brave soldier lost an arm in the battle.

51. ✘ The doctor says it is hopeless case.

✔ The doctor says it is a hopeless case.

52. ✘ She likes to live in an open air.

✔ She likes to live in the open air.

53. ✘ Get pound of sugar from nearest grocer.

✔ Get a pound of sugar from the nearest grocer.

54. ✘ Set back clock; it is hour too fast.

✔ Set back the clock, It is an hour too fast.

55. ✘ Draw map of India.

✔ Draw the map of India.

56. ✘ Have you never seen elephant?

✔ Have you never seen an elephant?

57. ✘ Do not look gift horse in mouth.

✔ Do not look a gift horse in the mouth.

58. ✘ Livingstone was great explorer.

✔ Livingstone was a great explorer.

59. ✘ Who wishes to take bath with me?

✔ Who wishes to take a bath with me?

60. ✘ The river was spanned by iron bridge.

✔ The river was spanned by an iron bridge.

61. ✘ Moon did not rise till after ten.

✔ The moon did not rise till after ten.

62. ✘ They started late in afternoon.

✔ They started late in the afternoon.

63. ✘ How little, in general, people know about sky!

✔ How little, in general, people know about the sky!

64. ✘ Scheme failed for want of support.

✔ The scheme failed for want of support.

65. ✘ Umbrella is of no avail against thunderstorm.

✔ An umbrella is of no avail against thunderstorm.

66. ✘ It was proudest moment of his life.

✔ It was the proudest moment of his life.

67. ✘ Andamans are group of islands in Bay of Bengal.

✔ The Andamans are a group of islands in the Bay of Bengal.

68. ✘ April is fourth month of the year.

✔ April is the fourth month of the year.

69. ✘ Dr. Arnold was headmaster of Rugby.

✔ Dr. Arnold was the headmaster of Rugby.

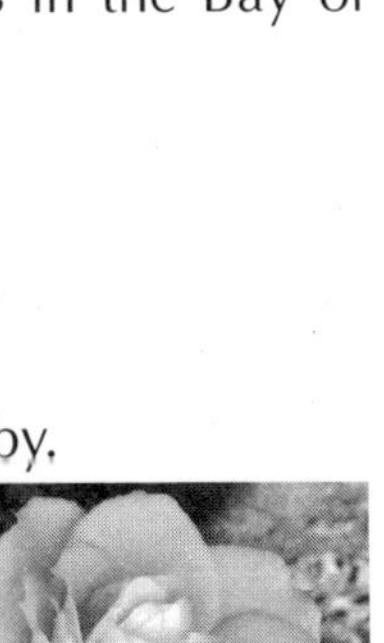

70. ✘ Wrap it in a envelope.

✔ Wrap it in an envelope.

71. ✘ Rose is beautiful flower.

✔ The rose is a beautiful flower.

72. ✘ Mayor inaugurated the function.

✔ The Mayor inaugurated the function.

73. ✘ Earth rotates on its axis.

✔ The earth rotates on its axis.

74. ✘ He has lot of work to do.

✔ He has a lot of work to do.

75. ✘ Himalayas are highest mountains.

✔ The Himalayas are the highest mountains.

76. ✘ Fool is led by nose.

✔ The fool is led by the nose.

77. ✘ He has Gita and Koran.

✔ He has the Gita and the Koran.

78. ✘ Taj is a historical monument.

✔ The Taj is a historical monument.

79. ✘ British live in Britain.

✔ The British live in Britain.

80. ✘ Higher you go cooler it is.

✔ The higher you go the cooler is it.

81. ✘ My cousin lives in U.S.A.

✔ My cousin lives in the U.S.A.

82. ✘ U.S.S.R. has disintegrated into C.I.S.

✔ The U.S.S.R. has disintegrated into C.I.S.

83. ✘ The man is a social animal.

✔ Man is a social animal.

84. ✘ Rich should help poor.

✔ The rich should help the poor.

85. ✘ Wanted a M.A. in English.

✔ Wanted an M.A. in English.

86. ✘ The Delhi is the capital of India.

✔ Delhi is the capital of India.

87. ✘ She is more clever of two sisters.

✔ She is more clever of the two sisters.

88. ✘ The both brothers are good actors.

✔ Both the brothers are good actors.

89. ✘ Elizabeth first died as a spinster.

✔ Elizabeth, the first died as a spinster.

90. ✘ Here is fifty-rupee note.

✔ Here is a fifty-rupee note.

91. ✘ These days, there is mad rush for making money.

✔ These days, there is a mad rush for making money.

92. ✘ Tradition of Diwali celebration is very old.

✔ The tradition of Diwali celebration is very old.

CLUES

1. 'A' and 'an' are called Indefinite Articles because they don't refer to any particular person or thing; as (i) A movie (any movie) (ii) A boy (any boy)
2. 'The' is called Definite Article as it points out some particular person or thing; as,

   I saw the movie : meaning that some particular movie.
3. Article 'an' is used before singular countable nouns beginning with vowels; as, an egg, an ox, an umbrella.
4. The choice between 'a' and 'an' is determined by sound. Thus, we say 'an hour', 'a union', 'a university', 'a European', 'a useful thing', 'a one-rupee note', 'a one-eyed man'.
5. We say 'an hour' because though 'h' is a consonant, it is not pronounced. Similarly, we say 'a European', because the pronunciation of the word 'European' is 'Yuropean' and as 'y' is a consonant, article 'a' is used.
6. The definite Article 'the' is used :

   When a particular person or thing is spoken of, or which has already been referred to; as,

   (i) He knows the way.

   (ii) The present you gave me is very beautiful.

   - When a singular Noun is meant to represent a whole class; as,

     The tiger is a fearless animal.

   - 'Man' and 'woman' when representing the whole class don't have either article; as,

     Man is born to experience joys and sorrows.

   - With names of rivers, seas, oceans, gulfs, group of islands and mountain ranges; as

     The Ganga, The Red Sea, The Alps

- Before the names of scriptures; as

  The Gita, the Mahabharata, the Ramayana.

- Before common nouns which are names of things unique of their kinds; as

  The earth, the sky, the moon, the sun.

- Before superlative degree of adjective; as

  He is the most intelligent boy of our class.

- Before ordinals; as

  The third chapter of this novel is full of interest

- Before musical instruments; as,

  I can play the guitar.

- Before an adjective when the noun is understood; as,

  The rich are not always happy.

- Before an adverb with comparative; as,

  The more you get, the more you want

omission of 'the' article

1. Before a Common Noun used in its widest sense; as,

   Men are mortal.

2. Before names of materials; as,

   Gold is a precious metal.

3. Before proper nouns; as,

   Kolkata is the capital of West Bengal.

   Note : When 'the' article is used before proper nouns, they become common nouns; as,

   Kalidas is the Shakespeare of India.

4. Before abstract Nouns used in general sense; as,

    Honesty is the best policy.

    Note : When an Abstract noun is qualified by an Adjective phrase, it may have 'the' article; as,

    The wisdom of Shakespeare is well known.

5. Before languages; as,

    We are studying French.

6. Before college school, church, table, bed, hospital, market prison; as,

    He has been admitted in hospital.

    We go to church on Sunday.

    Note : 'the' article is used with these words when they are referred as definite, as,

    I went to see him in the hospital.

7. Before names of relations; as,

    Mother, father aunt, uncle

8. Before Predicative noun denoting a position held at one time by one person; as,

    He was elected director of the Board.

9. In certain phrases consisting of Transitive Verb followed by its object, as

    to set sail, to lose heart, to leave office, to give ear, to catch fire.

10. In certain phrases consisting of prepositions followed by their objects; as,

    at sunset, at lunch, by air, on foot, under ground, on ground, at break.

8

Modal Auxiliaries

Carefully study the following sentences in order to know why errors creep in the use of modals :

1. ✗ *Can* I come in sir?
   ✓ *May* I come in sir?
2. ✗ *May* you lift this heavy box?
   ✓ *Can* you lift this heavy box?
3. ✗ He *may* work this sum.
   ✓ He *can* work this sum.
4. ✗ I *may* swim across the river.
   ✓ I *can* swim across the river.

5. ✗ It *can* rain tomorrow.
   ✓ It *may* rain tomorrow.
6. ✗ She *can* be at home.
   ✓ She *may* be at home.
7. ✗ *May* this be true?
   ✓ *Can* this be true?
8. ✗ It *may* not be true.
   ✓ It *can* not be true.

9. ✗ You *may* live happily and long!
   ✔ *May* you live happily and long!
10. ✗ Success may attend you!
    ✔ May success attend you!
11. ✗ She *can* swim across the river when she was young.
    ✔ She *could* swim across the river when she was young.

12. ✗ He said I *may* go.
    ✔ He said I *might* go.
13. ✗ I thought she *may* be at home.
    ✔ I thought she *might* be at home.
14. ✗ I wondered whether it *can* be true.
    ✔ I wondered whether it could be true.
15. ✗ *Can* you pass me the salt?
    ✔ Could you pass me the salt?
16. ✗ You *may* pay a little more attention to your appearance.
    ✔ You might pay a little more attention to your appearance.
17. ✗ I *will* be fifty five next birthday.
    ✔ I *shall* be fifty five next birthday.
18. ✗ Yesterday I *could* swim across the river.
    ✔ Yesterday I *was able* to swim across the river.
19. ✗ When *will* we see you again?
    ✔ When *shall* we see you again?
20. ✗ Tomorrow *will* be Monday.
    ✔ Tomorrow *shall* be Monday.
21. ✗ You *shall* see that I am right.
    ✔ You *will* see that I am right.
22. ✗ He *will* not enter my house again.
    ✔ He *shall* not enter my house again.

23. ✘ You *will* have a holiday tomorrow.

✔ You *shall* have a holiday tomorrow.

24. ✘ You *will* be punished for this.

✔ You *shall* be punished for this.

25. ✘ *Will* I open the door?

✔ *Shall* I open the door?

26. ✘ Which book *will* I buy ?

✔ Which book shall I buy?

27. ✘ *Will* the waiter serve food now?

✔ *Shall* the waiter serve food now?

28. ✘ I *shall* carry your box.

✔ I *will* carry your box.

29. ✘ I *shall* try to do better next time.

✔ I *will* try to do better next time.

30. ✘ I *shall* succeed or die in the attempt.

✔ I *will* succeed or die in the attempt.

31. ✘ She *shall* talk about nothing but films.

✔ She *will* talk about nothing but films.

32. ✘ He *shall* sit for hours listening to the music.

✔ He *will* sit for hours listening to the music.

33. ✘ This *shall* be the pen you want, I suppose.

✔ This *will* be the pen you want, I suppose.

34. ✘ That *shall* be the postmaster, I think.

✔ That *will* be the postmaster, I think.

35. ✘ *Shall* you have tea?

✔ *Will* you have tea?

36. ✘ *Shall* you lend me your computer?

✔ *Will* you lend me your computer?

37. ✘ I expected that I *shall* get a first class.

✔ I expected that I *should* (more often: would) get a first class.

38. ✘ He said he *will* be fifty five next birthday.

✔ He said he *would* be fifty five next birthday

39. ✘ She said she *will* carry my books.

✔ She said she *would* carry my books.

40. ✘ She *will* sit for hours listening to the music.

✔ She *would* sit for hours listening to the music.

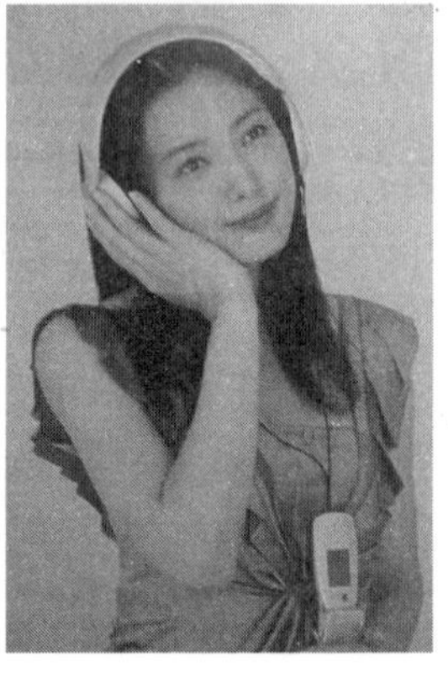

41. ✘ We *shall* obey the laws.

✔ We *should* obey the laws.

42. ✘ You *shall* keep your promise.

✔ You *should* keep your promise.

43. ✘ Children *will* obey their parents.

✔ Children *should* obey their parents.

44. ✘ If it *shall* rain, he will not come.

✔ If it *should* rain he will not come.

45. ✘ If she *will* see me here, she will be happy.

✔ If she should see me here, she will be happy.

46. ✘ I *shall* like you to help her.

✔ I *should/would* like you to help her.

47. ✘ *Will* you lend me your computer please?

✔ *Would* you lend me your computer please?

48. ✘ You *shall* have been more careful.

✔ You *should* have been more careful.

49. ✗ He *shall* be in the library now.

✔ He *should* be in the library now.

50. ✗ I wish you *could* come to deliver the message personally.

✔ I wish you *would* come to deliver the message personally.

51. ✗ You *should* work or starve.

✔ You *must* work or starve.

52. ✗ We *would* obey the laws.

✔ We *must* obey the laws.

53. ✗ I *should* have my way in this matter.

✔ I *must* have my way in this matter.

54. ✗ You *should* be fifty now.

✔ You *must* be fifty now.

55. ✗ We *must* love our neighbours.

✔ We *ought* to love our neighbours.

56. ✗ We *must* help him.

✔ We ought to help him.

57. ✗ You *must* know better.

✔ You *ought to* know better.

58. ✗ Sita *must* win.

✔ Sita *ought to* win.

59. ✗ The film *may* be a great success.

✔ The film *ought to be* a great success.

60. ✗ I *would* live there when I was young.

✔ I used to live there when I was young.

61. ✗ There *would* be a house here.

✔ There *used to* be a house here.

62. ✗ He *needs* not go.

✔ He *need* not go.

63. ✗ I hardly *need* take his help.

✔ I *need* hardly take his help.

64. ✗ He *dares* not take such a step.

✔ He *dare* not take such a step.

65. ✗ How do you dare to contradict me?

✔ How *dare* you contradict me?

CLUES

1 'May' is used to express permission 2-4, 'Can' expresses ability or capacity 5-6, 'May' is used to express possibility in affirmative sentences 7-8, 'Can' is used in the corresponding interrogative and negative sentences 9-10, 'May' is also used to express a wish 11-14, 'Could' and 'Might' are used as the past equivalent of 'Can' and 'May'.

15 (polite request) 16, 'Might' is also used to express a degree of dissatisfaction or reproach 17, 'Shall' is used in the first person to express pure future 18. You should not say 'yesterday I could swim across the river'; should say 'yesterday I was able to swim across the river'.

19-21, 'Will' is used in the second and third persons to express pure future 22-24, 'Shall is used in the second and third persons to express a command, a promise or threat 23-27, 'Shall' is used in the second and third persons to ask after the will of the person addressed 28-30, Will' is used to express volition 31-32, 'Will' is also used to express characteristic habit 33-34, 'Will' is also used to express assumption or probability 35-36, 'Will you' indicates an invitation or request 37-40, 'Should' and 'would' are used as the past equivalents of 'shall' and 'will' 41-43, 'Should' is used in all persons to express duty or obligation 44-45. In clauses of condition 'Should' is used to express a supposition that may not be true 46, 'Should/Would like' is a polite form of want 47, 'would you'? is more polite than 'will you'? 48, 'should+perfect infinitive' indicates a past obligation that was not fulfilled 49, 'should be' here expresses probability 50, 'Would' after 'wish' expresses a strong desire 51-52, 'Must' expresses necessity or obligation 53-54, 'must' also expresses determination 55-57, 'ought (to)' expresses moral obligation or desirability 58-59, 'ought (to)' may also express strong probability 60-61, 'used to' expresses a discontinued habit 62-63. The auxiliary 'need', denoting neccesity or obligation, can be conjugated with or without 'do'. When conjugated without 'do', it has no -s and -ed forms and is used with an infinitive without 'to' only in negative and interrogative sentences and in sentences that contain-semi-negative words like 'scarcity' and 'hardly' 64-65. The auxiliary 'dare' does not take - 's' on the third person singular present tense. It is generally used in negative and interrogative sentences. When conjugated without 'do', it is followed by an infinitive without to; when conjugated with 'do', it takes an infinitive with or without 'to', after it.

9

Erroneous Agreement of the Verb with the Subject

The verb should agree with its subject in person and number — singular or plural. Errors creep in when verbs fail to agree with their subjects. Therefore it is important to identify the subject and its number and then it is made to agree with the verb. An unwary person may not be able to find out the right subject and number and may thus create errors in writing or speaking.

Study the following sentences carefully so as to avoid errors arising out of the wrong subject verb concord :

1. ✘ My friend and guide are attending the meeting.
   ✔ My friend and guide is attending the meeting.
2. ✘ The captain and officer commanding have arrived.
   ✔ The captain and officer commanding has arrived..
3. ✘ My friend and benefactor have come.
   ✔ My friend and benefactor has come.
4. ✘ The orator and author are dead.
   ✔ The orator and author is dead.
5. ✘ The captain and adjutant were present.
   ✔ The captain and adjutant was present.

CLUES

Agreement of the verb with the subject.

(i) When two singular Nouns refer to the same person or thing, the verb must be singular.

Also notice that article 'the' is used only once when the two nouns refer to the same person.

(ii) In the above sentences(1-5) (1) My friend and guide (2) Captain and officer commanding (3) My friend and benefactor (4) orator and author (5) Captain and adjutant are the same persons.

6. ✗ Bread and milk are my only food.

   ✔ Bread and milk is my only food.

7. ✗ The horse and the carriage are at the door.

   ✔ The horse and carriage is at the door.

8. ✗ The long and short of the matter are this.

   ✔ The long and short of the matter is this.

9. ✗ Slow and steady win the race.

   ✔ Slow and steady wins the race.

CLUES

In the above sentences - 6 to 9, the two objects together express one idea and hence the verb is singular.

10. ✗ Every boy and girl are ready.

    ✔ Every boy and girl is ready.

11. ✘ Each day and each hour bring its duty.
    ✔ Each day and each hour brings its duty.
12. ✘ Every man, woman and child were saved.
    ✔ Every man, woman and child was saved.
13. ✘ Every man and woman of the town were present at the festival.
    ✔ Every man and woman of the town was present at the festival.
14. ✘ Each day and each night add to his worries.
    ✔ Each day and each night adds to his worries.

CLUES

In the above sentences (10-14) the verb is singular because if the singular subjects are preceded by *each* or *every*, the verb is usually singular.

15. ✘ No nook or corner were left unexplored.
    ✔ No nook or corner was left unexplored.
16. ✘ Neither he or I were there.
    ✔ Neither he nor I was there.
17. ✘ Either Arun or Hari had stolen the watch.
    ✔ Either Arun or Hari has stolen the watch.
18. ✘ Neither Darcy nor his sister were there.
    ✔ Neither Darcy nor his sister was there.
19. ✘ Neither food nor water were to be found there.
    ✔ Neither food nor water was to be found there.
20. ✘ Neither blame nor praise seem to affect him.
    ✔ Neither blame nor praise seems to affect him.
21. ✘ Neither you nor your friend were present.
    ✔ Neither you nor your friend was present.
22. ✘ Either you or your daughter have stolen the purse.
    ✔ Either you or your daughter has stolen the purse.

23. ✘ No man or woman were left unattended.

✔ No man or woman was left unattended.

CLUES

Two or more singular subjects connected by *or, nor, either, ... or, neither,....* nor take a verb in the singular. Hence the above sentences - (15-23) should take singular verbs.

24. ✘ John or his parents has done this.

✔ John or his parents have done this.

25. ✘ Neither the principal nor the teachers was present.

✔ Neither the principal nor the teachers were present.

26. ✘ Neither Johnson nor his colleagues was hurt.

✔ Neither Johnson nor his colleagues were hurt.

27. ✘ Either the girl or her parents has erred.

✔ Either the girl or her parents have erred.

CLUES

When the subject joined by *or,* nor are of different persons, the verb must be plural and the plural subject must be placed before the verb. Hence the above sentences 24-27 have plural verbs and plural subject are placed before the verbs.

28. ✘ Either he or I are mistaken.

✔ Either he or I am mistaken.

29. ✘ Neither he or his friend are to blame.

✔ Neither he or his friend is to blame.

CLUES

When the subjects joined by *or, nor* are of different persons, the verb agrees in person with the one nearest to it.

30. ✘ He and I am well.

✔ He and I are well.

31. ✘ I and my father has lived here for three years.

✔ I and my father have lived here for three years.

32. ✘ You and he is birds of the same feather.

✔ You and he are birds of the same feather.

33. ✘ You and I has done our duty.

✔ You and I have done our duty.

CLUES

When subjects differing in number, or person or both, are connected by '*and*', the verb must always be in plural; and of the First Person, if one of the subjects is of that person; of the second person, if one of the subjects is of that person, and none of the first

34. ✘ The council have chosen its president.

✔ The council has chosen its president.

35. ✘ The fleet have set sail.

✔ The fleet has set sail.

36. ✘ In regards to details, the committee was divided.

✔ In regards to details, the committee were divided.

37. ✘ There are a large number of students in this class.

✔ There is a large number of students in this class.

38. ✘ The mob have set the house on fire.

✔ The mob has set the house on fire.

39. ✘ Parliament have elected its Speaker.

✔ Parliament has elected its Speaker.

40. ✘ The majority are against any compromise.

✔ The majority is against any compromise.

41. ✘ A number of interesting suggestions has been made.

✔ A number of interesting suggestions have been made.

42. ✘ The military was called out.

✔ The military were called out.

43. ✘ The crew were large.

✔ The crew was large.

44. ✘ The crew was taken prisoners.

✔ The crew were taken prisoners.

45. ✘ At first the jury were divided in opinion, but finally it gave a unanimous verdict.

✔ At first the jury were divided in opinion, but finally they gave a unanimous verdict.

CLUES

A collective noun takes a singular verb when the collection is thought of as a whole; a plural verb when the individuals of which it is composed, are thought of.

46. ✘ The news are true.

✔ The news is true.

47. ✘ Mathematics are a branch of study in every school.

✔ Mathematics is a branch of study in every school.

48. ✘ The wages of sin are death.

✔ The wages of sin is death.

49. ✘ Politics were with her the business of her life.

✔ Politics was with her the business of her life.

CLUES

Some nouns as given above are plural in form but singular in meaning, take a singular verb.

50. ✘ According to the present market rate twelve dozen costs two hundred rupees.

✔ According to the present market rate twelve dozen cost two hundred rupees.

CLUES

Some nouns such as 'dozen' which are singular in form but plural in meaning, take a plural verb.

51. ✘ Each of the brothers are clever.

✔ Each of the brothers is clever.

52. ✘ Each of the girls were given a prize.

✔ Each of the girls was given a prize.

53. ✘ Neither of the boys were very tall.

✔ Neither of the boys was very tall.

54. 8 Each of these substances are found in India.

✔ Each of these substances is found in India.

55. ✘ Each one of their houses are to let.

✔ Each one of their houses is to let.

56. ✘ A variety of pleasing objects charm the eye.

✔ A variety of pleasing objects charms the eye.

57. ✘ The quality of the oranges were not good.

✔ The quality of the oranges was not good.

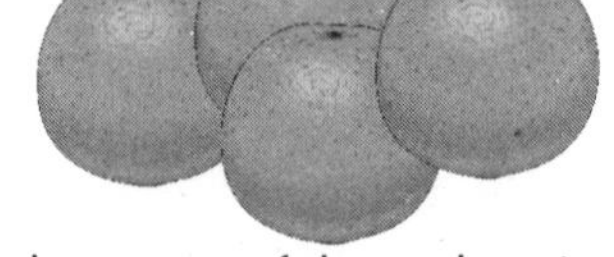

58. ✘ If it were possible to get near when one of the volcanic eruptions take place, one should see a great sight.

✔ If it were possible to get near when one of the volcanic eruptions takes place, one should see a great sight.

CLUES

When a plural noun comes between a singular subject and its verb, the verb should not be wrongly made to agree with the nearest plural noun, but with the real subject.

59. ✘ The commander, with all his soldiers were killed.

✔ The commander, with all his soldiers was killed.

60. ✘ The governor, with his aide-de-camp have arrived.

61 ✘ The governor, with his aide-de-camp has arrived.

62. ✘ Justice as well as mercy allow it.

✔ Justice as well as mercy allows it.

63. ✘ Johan as well as Philips deserve praise.

✔ Johan as well as Philips deserves praise.

64. ✘ Sita, as well as Gita and Rita, like mangoes.

✔ Sita, as well as Gita and Rita likes mangoes.

65. ✘ Darcy, and not you, have done this.

✔ Darcy, and not you, has done this.

CLUES

Words joined to a singular subject by *'with', 'together with', 'in addition to',* or *'as well as'* etc are parenthetical, and therefore do not affect the number of the verb.

66. ✘ I who is your friend, will guard your interests.

✔ I who am your friend will guard your interests.

67. ✘ You, who is my son, should not bother me.

✔ You, who are my son, should not bother me.

68. ✘ She who are my friend, should stand by me.

✔ She who is my friend should stand by me.

69. ✘ She is one the best mothers that has ever lived.

✔ She is one of the best mothers that have ever lived.

CLUES

When the subject of the verb is a relative pronoun, the verb should agree in number and person with the antecedent of the relative.

10

Pitfalls in the Use of Preposition

A preposition is a word placed before a noun or a pronoun to show in what relation the person or thing denoted by it stands in regard to something else.

The word preposition means "that which is placed before".

A preposition is usually placed before its object, but sometimes it follows it.

Prepositions are simple but sometimes proper use and placing of prepositions pose a problem.

Note the following sentences to know the proper use of prepositions.

1. ✘ The goat subsists *at* the coarsest food.
   ✔ The goat subsists *on* the coarsest food.
2. ✘ Jaunpur is famous *in* its perfumes.
   ✔ Jaunpur is famous *for* its perfumes.
3. ✘ India is teeming *at* natural wealth.
   ✔ India is teeming with natural wealth.
4. ✘ Many Mughal kings were fond *for* architecture.
   ✔ Many Mughal kings were fond *of* architecture.
5. ✘ In the classical age, the ideal life of the Brahman was divided *in* four stages.

✔ In the classical age, the ideal life of the Brahman was divided *into* four stages.

6. ✘ It is natural in every man to wish *of* distinction.

   ✔ It is natural in every man to wish *for* distinction.

7. ✘ The prince was endowed *in* many gifts.

   ✔ The prince was endowed *with* many gifts.

8. ✘ The writer is evidently enamoured *in* the subject.

   ✔ The writer is evidently enamoured *of* the subject.

9. ✘ This temple is not inaccessible *for* strangers.

   ✔ This temple is not inaccessible *to* strangers.

10. ✘ Ambition does not always conduce *for* lasting happiness.

    ✔ Ambition does not always conduce *to* lasting happiness.

11. ✘ This person is affable for his colleagues.

    ✔ This person is affable to his colleagues.

12. ✘ Newly acquired freedom is sometimes liable *for* abuse.

    ✔ Newly acquired freedom is sometimes liable to abuse.

13. ✘ The angel proved quite a match *against* the giant.

    ✔ The angel proved quite a match *for* the giant.

14. ✘ He is confined *with* the forewalls of the house.

    ✔ He is confined *to* the forewalls of the house.

15. ✘ Camels are strangely adapted *at* life in the desert.

    ✔ Camels are strangely adapted *to* life in the desert.

16. ✘ A foolish is generally ignorant *at* his follies.

    ✔ A foolish is generally ignorant *of* his follies.

17. ✘ The income derived *of* the ownership of land is commonly called rent.

    ✔ The income derived *from* the ownership of land is commonly called rent.

18. ✘ This person is famous *in* his learning.

✔ This person is famous *for* his learning.

19. ✘ Alexander profited *at* the dissensions of the Rajas of Punjab.

✔ Alexander profited *by* the dissensions of the Rajas of Punjab.

20. ✘ Nothing is impossible *for* skill and diligence.

✔ Nothing is impossible *to* skill and diligence.

21. ✘ I am greatly indebted *of* my parents.

✔ I am greatly indebted *to* my parents.

22. ✘ We should be tolerant *in* all religions.

✔ We should be tolerant *of* all religions.

23. ✘ Patanjali was a contemporary *from* Pushyamitra.

✔ Patanjali was a contemporary *of* Pushyamitra.

24. ✘ We should adapt ourselves *at* changed circumstances.

✔ We should adapt ourselves *to* changed circumstances.

25. ✘ Wordsworth's poetry is remarkable *at* the perfection of its execution.

✔ Wordsworth's poetry is remarkable *for* the perfection of its execution.

26. ✘ Every quality peculiar *of* the Saxons was hateful to the Britons.

✔ Every quality peculiar *to* the Saxons was hateful to the Britons.

27. ✘ You should acquaint yourself *at* the working of this office.

✔ You should acquaint yourself *with* the working of this office.

28. ✘ He does not associate *in* ignoble persons.

✔ He does not associate with ignoble persons.

29. ✘ Your duties are of a kind ill-suited *for* your ardent and daring character.

✔ Your duties are of a kind ill-suited *to* your ardent and daring character.

30. ✘ This answer is entirely different *than* the other answer.

✔ This answer is entirely different *from* the other answer.

31. ✘ He seems to be addicted *with* the bottle.

✔ He seems to be addicted *to* the bottle.

32. ✘ She is somewhat susceptible *for* flattery.

✔ She is somewhat susceptible *to* flattery.

33. ✘ A man who always connives *with* the faults of his children is their worst enemy.

✔ A man who always connives *at* the faults of his children is their worst enemy.

34. ✘ Naples was then destitute *at* what are now, perhaps, its chief attractions.

✔ Naples was then destitute *of* what are now, perhaps, its chief attractions.

35. ✘ This custom seems to have originated *at* the East.

✔ This custom seems to have originated *in* the East.

36. ✘ Judged *from* its results, the policy of Akbar was successful.

✔ Judged *by* its results, the policy of Akbar was successful.

37. ✘ You had hinted *about* the forthcoming events.

✔ You had hinted *at* the forthcoming events.

38. ✘ Quinine acts as a preventive *to* malaria.

✔ Quinine act as a preventive *of* malaria.

39. ✘ If you are averse *with* hardwork, you will not succeed in life.

✔ If you are averse *to* hardwork, you will not succeed in life.

40. ✘ It was formerly supposed that malaria was due *from* poisonous exhalations.

✔ It was formerly supposed that malaria was due to poisonous exhalations.

41. ✘ Many persons were afflicted *by* leprosy.

✔ May persons were afflicated *with* leprosy.

42. ✘ You should speak something appropriate *for* the occasion.

✔ You should speak something appropriate *to* the occasion.

43. ✘ We should abstain *of* animal food.

✔ We should abstain *from* animal food.

44. ✘ He has antipathy *for* dogs.

✔ He has antipathy *to* dogs.

45. ✘ This herb is beneficial *for* health.

✔ This herb is beneficial *to* health.

46. ✘ Very few persons were worthy *at* praise.

✔ Very few persons were worthy *of* praise.

47. ✘ We are accountable *with* God for our deeds.

✔ We are accountable *to* God for our deeds.

48. ✘ He has no aptitude *in* business.

✔ He has no aptitude *for* business.

49. ✘ We must all atone *with* our misdeeds.

✔ We must all atone *for* our misdeeds.

50. ✘ Many persons are getting addicted *for* alcohol.

✔ Many persons are getting addicted *to* alcohol.

51. ✘ He has become indifferent *for* praise or blame.

✔ He has become indifferent *to* praise or blame.

52. ✘ In this office, there is no incentive *for* hardwork.

✔ In this office, there is no incentive *to* hardwork.

53. ✘ You should not be heedless *for* consequences.

✔ You should not be heedless *of* consequences.

54. ✘ All the guests convulsed *for* laughter.

✔ All the guests convulsed *with* laughter.

55. ✘ The dictator was deaf *for* entreaties of the poor.

✔ The dictator was deaf *to* entreaties of the poor.

56. ✘ On seeing the plight of the children, all were touched *for* pity.

✔ On seeing the plight of the children, all were touched *with* pity.

57. ✘ Some people are very sensitive *for* criticism.

✔ Some people are very sensitive *to* criticism.

CLUES

The Verbs, Nouns, Adjectives and Participles given in the foregoing sentences are always followed by particular prepositions as used with them.

58. ✘ Parents have affection *with* their children.

✔ Parents have affection *for* their children.

59. ✘ He has ambition *in* army.

✔ He has ambition *for* army.

60. ✘ You have no anxiety *of* your sick mother.

✔ You have no anxiety *for* your sick mother.

61. ✘ You must have capacity *of* hardwork.

✔ You must have capacity *for* hardwork.

62. ✘ We must have compassion *with* the poor.

✔ We must have compassion *for* the poor.

63. ✘ Children have fondness *of* animals.

✔ Children have fondness *for* animals.

64. ✘ The tyrant had no pity *with* the orphans.

✔ The tyrant had no pity *for* the orphans.

65. ✘ You shall get guarantee *with* this product.

✔ You shall get guarantee *for* this product.

66. ✘ One should not have partiality *with* the people of any caste, religion or creed.

✔ One should not have partiality *for* the people of any caste, religion or creed.

67. ✘ This boy is a good match *of* your daughter.

✔ This boy is a good match *for* your daughter.

68. ✘ All have desire *to* knowledge.

✔ All have desire *for* knowledge.

69. ✘ Boys have fondness *with* dogs.

✔ Boys have fondness *for* dogs.

70. ✘ The accused has no remorse *with* the crime done by him.

✔ The accused has no remorse *for* the crime done by him.

71. ✘ This is a good opportunity *of* repentence.

✔ This is a good opportunity *for* repentence.

72. ✘ He has no fondness *of* music.

✔ He has no fondness *for* music.

73. ✘ I have passion *at* driving.

✔ I have passion *for* driving.

CLUES

The above Nouns take the preposition *'for'* after them.

74. ✗ I have no acquaintance *in* these persons.
    ✔ I have no acquaintance *with* these persons.
75. ✗ India has entered into alliance *for* the neighbouring countries.
    ✔ India has entered into alliance *with* the neighbouring countries. 
76. ✗ You cannot bargain *at* every seller.
    ✔ You cannot bargain *with* every seller.
77. ✗ You have no comparison *at* him.
    ✔ You have no comparison *with* him.
78. ✗ His answer is not in conformity *at* the question.
    ✔ His answer is not in conformity *with* the question.
79. ✗ I have no enmity *for* any one.
    ✔ I have no enmity *with* any one.
80. ✗ Darcy has close intimacy *for* all the people in this area.
    ✔ Darcy has close intimacy *with* all the people in this area.
81. ✗ Don't keep relations *for* any one here.
    ✔ Don't keep relations *with* any one here.

CLUES

The above Nouns take the preposition *'with'* after them.

82. ✗ Children have abhorrence *with* bees.
    ✔ Children have abhorrence *for* bees.
83. ✗ Provide a strong proof *for* your ignorance.
    ✔ Provide a strong proof *of* your ignorance.

84. ✘ What is the result *for* your hardwork?

✔ What is the result *of* your hardwork?

85. ✘ He gave me an assurance *for* help.

✔ He gave me an assurance *of* help.

86. ✘ You can take change *at* office.

✔ You can take change *of* office.

87. ✘ This candidate has no experience *for* work.

✔ This candidate has no experience *of* work.

88. ✘ There is a strong doubt *at* negligence.

✔ There is a strong doubt *of* negligence.

89. ✘ A strong want *for* cold water is being expressed.

✔ A strong want *of* cold water is being expressed.

CLUES

The above Nouns take the preposition '*of*' after them.

90. ✘ Only select persons have access of this well.

✔ Only select persons have access to this well.

91. ✘ The accession of throne is subject to many conditions.

✔ The accession to throne is subject to many conditions.

92. ✘ I owe my allegiance for the principal.

✔ I owe my allegiance to the principal.

93. ✘ You have no approach *at* the headoffice.

✔ You have no approach *to* the headoffice.

94. ✘ Some students have antipathy *for* the homework.

✔ Some students have antipathy *to* the homework.

95. ✘ She has no approach *at* the police commissioner.

✔ The has no approach *to* the police commissioner.

96. ✘ The chairman gave assent *for* our proposal.

✔ The chairman gave assent *to* our proposal.

97. ✘ You seem to have no attachment *with* this area.

✔ You seem to have no attachment *to* this area.

98. ✘ Pay attention *for* what I say.

✔ Pay attention *to* what I say.

99. ✘ He is a disgrace *for* his family.

✔ He is a disgrace *to* his family.

100. ✘ Boys have a strong dislike *for* work.

✔ Boys have a strong dislike *to* work.

101. ✘ The military provided encouragement *for* one and all.

✔ The military provided encouragement *to* one and all.

102. ✘ There is no exception *on* this rule.

✔ There is no exception *to* this rule.

103. ✘ We gave invitation *for* every one.

✔ We gave invitation *to* every one.

104. ✘ There is no incentive *for* hard work.

✔ There is no incentive *to* hard work.

105. ✘ He showed indifference *for* every thing.

✔ He showed indifference *to* every thing.

106. ✘ Don't show leniency *for* children.

✔ Don't show leniency *to* children.

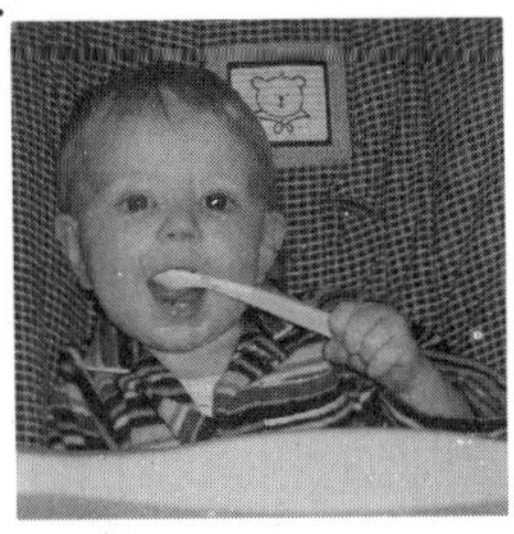

107. ✘ There is a limit *for* tolerance.

✔ There is a limit *to* tolerance.

108. ✘ This boy is a menace *for* the family.

✔ This boy is a menace *to* the family.

109. ✘ Obedience *for* rules is must.

✔ Obedience *to* rules is must.

110. ✘ There is no objection *at* your sitting here.

✔ There is no objection *to* your sitting here.

111. ✘ There was a strong opposition *for* this proposal.

✔ There was a strong opposition *to* this proposal.

112. ✘ Don't be an obstruction *at* work.

✔ Don't be an obstruction *to* work.

113. ✘ The boy has resemblance *for* his mother.

✔ The boy has resemblance *to* his mother.

114. ✘ Please write a preface *for* the book.

✔ Please write a preface *to* the book

115. ✘ He gave reference *of* his father's education.

✔ He gave reference *to* his father's education.

116. ✘ The prince's succession *of* throne was delayed.

✔ The prince's succession *to* throne was delayed

117. ✘ He has temptation *for* alcohol.

✔ He has temptation *to* alcohol.

118. ✘ No one should prove himself a traitor *for* his country.

✔ No one should prove himself a traitor *to* his country.

CLUES

The above Nouns take the preposition *'to'* after them.

119. ✘ Abstinence *of* alcohol will improve your health.

✔ Abstinence *from* alcohol will improve your health.

120. ✘ The Almighty can provide deliverance *off* sorrows.

✔ The Almighty can provide deliverance *from* sorrows.

121. ✘ His descent is *of* noble family.

✔ His descent is *from* noble family.

122. ✘ There is no escape *for* death.

✔ There is no escape *from* death.

123. ✘ He got exemption *at* appearing in the interview.

✔ He got exemption *from* appearing in the interview.

124. ✘ There is no respite *in* the strong heat.

✔ There is no respite *from* the strong heat.

CLUES

The above Nouns take the preposition 'from' after them.

125. ✘ The proposal is not acceptable *for* us.

✔ The proposal is not acceptable *to* us.

126. ✘ I am not accustomed *for* this type of atmosphere.

✔ I am not accustomed *to* this type of atmosphere.

127. ✘ Don't get addicted *for* alcohol.

✔ Don't get addicted *to* alcohol.

128. ✘ He lives adjacent *for* my house.

✔ He lives adjacent *to* my house.

129. ✘ You are affectionate *for* your parents.

✔ You are affectionate *to* your parents.

130. ✘ This decision is not agreeable *for* our proposal.

✔ This decision is not agreeable *to* our proposal.

131. ✘ An animal akin *of* tiger inhabits this area.

✔ An animal akin *to* tiger inhabits this area.

132. ✘ I am an alien *for* this place.

✔ I am an alien *to* this place.

133. ✘ You should be alive *for* the problems of life.
✔ You should be alive *to* the problems of life.

134. ✘ Your answer is not appropriate *for* the occasion.
✔ Your answer is not appropriate *to* the occasion.

135. ✘ This herb is beneficial *for* health.
✔ This herb is beneficial *to* health.

136. ✘ Don't remain callous *for* the problems of the poor.
✔ Don't remain callous *to* the problems of the poor.

137. ✘ Your answer is not comparable *with* his answer.
✔ Your answer is not comparable *to* his answer.

138. ✘ The accused is condemned *for* death.
✔ The accused is condemned *to* death.

139. ✘ This place is congenial *for* our health.
✔ This place is congenial *to* our health.

140. ✘ The result is contrary *of* my expectations.
✔ The result is contrary *to* my expectations.

141. ✘ The tyrant remained deaf *on* our entreaties.
✔ The tyrant remained deaf *to* our entreaties.

142. ✘ Working in this factory is detrimental *for* health.
✔ Working in this factory is detrimental *to* health.

143. ✘ You should be devoted *in* your work.
✔ You should be devoted *to* your work.

144. ✘ The consequences of your deeds shall be disastrous *for* your life.
✔ The consequences of your deeds shall be disastrous *to* your life.

145. ✘ The dog is faithful *for* his master.
✔ The dog is faithful *to* his master.

146. ✘ You seem to be foreign *at* this place.

✔ You seem to be foreign *to* this place.

147. ✘ He is hostile *for* any request for reconciliation.

✔ He is hostile *to* any request for reconciliation.

148. ✘ This amount is due *for* him.

✔ This amount is due *to* him.

149. ✘ Exercise is essential *for* health.

✔ Exercise is essential *to* health.

150. ✘ Your life is exposed *in* so many dangers.

✔ Your life is exposed *to* so many dangers.

151. ✘ One should be faithful *in* one's duties.

✔ One should be faithful *to* one's duties.

152. ✘ Climate is inclined *for* change.

✔ Climate is inclined *to* change.

153. ✘ This medicine is impertinent *for* health.

✔ This medicine is impertinent *to* health.

154. ✘ He remained indifferent *at* our requests.

✔ He remained indifferent *to* our requests.

155. ✘ I shall remain indebted *in* you for your help.

✔ I shall remain indebted *to* you for your help.

156. ✘ Life-saving drugs are indispensable *for* health.

✔ Life-saving drugs are indispensable *to* health.

157. ✘ She is insensible *at* our problems.

✔ She is insensible *to* our problems.

158. ✘ Your answer is irrelavant *for* the asked question.

✔ Your answer is irrelavant *to* the asked question.

159. ✘ The climate of this place is favourable *for* health.

✔ The climate of this place is favourable *to* health.

160. ✘ Your action is favourable *for* our requirement.

✔ Your action is favourable *to* our requirement.

161. ✘ This type of light is hurtful *for* eyes.

✔ This type of light is hurtful *to* eyes.

162. ✘ Your answer is immaterial *for* our needs.

✔ Your answer is immaterial *to* our needs.

163. ✘ The courtiers were loyal *for* the king.

✔ The courtiers were loyal *to* the king.

164. ✘ Students should be obedient *for* teachers.

✔ Students should be obedient *to* teachers.

165. ✘ I am obliged *at* Indian Air Force.

✔ I am obliged *to* Indian Air Force.

166. ✘ You should not be partial *for* any one.

✔ You should not be partial *to* any one.

167. ✘ This curve is prone *for* accidents.

✔ This curve is prone *to* accidents.

168. ✘ The huge building was reduced *in* rubbles.

✔ The huge building was reduced *to* rubbles.

169. ✘ You are responsible *for* the chief executive.

✔ You are responsible *to* the chief executive.

170. ✘ Cold drink is preferable *for* hot tea.

✔ Cold drink is preferable *to* hot tea.

171. ✘ Your action is tantamount *for* punishment.

✔ Your action is tantamount *to* punishment.

172. ✘ His activities are restricted *at* this area.

✔ His activities are restricted *to* this area.

173. ✗ The awards were distributed prior *at* your arrival.

✔ The awards were distributed prior *to* your arrival.

174. ✗ You can be granted leave subject *for* the availability of manpower.

✔ You can be granted leave subject *to* the availability of manpower.

175. ✗ He is true *for* his word.

✔ He is true *to* his word.

CLUES

The above Adjectives and Participles take the preposition *'to'* after them.

176. ✗ Your song is not suitable *for* the occasion.

✔ Your song is not suitable *to* the occasion.

177. ✗ This fruit is deficient *of* proteins.

✔ This fruit is deficient *in* proteins.

178. ✗ They are involved *at* research.

✔ They are involved *in* research.

179. ✗ This man is interested *with* hardwork.

✔ This man is interested *in* hardwork.

180. ✗ You are proficient *at* mathematics.

✔ You are proficient *in* mathematics.

181. ✗ The teacher is well-versed *at* his subject.

✔ The teacher is well-versed *in* his subject.

182. ✗ The architect is accomplished *to* the work of architecture.

✔ The architect is accomplished *in* the work of architecture.

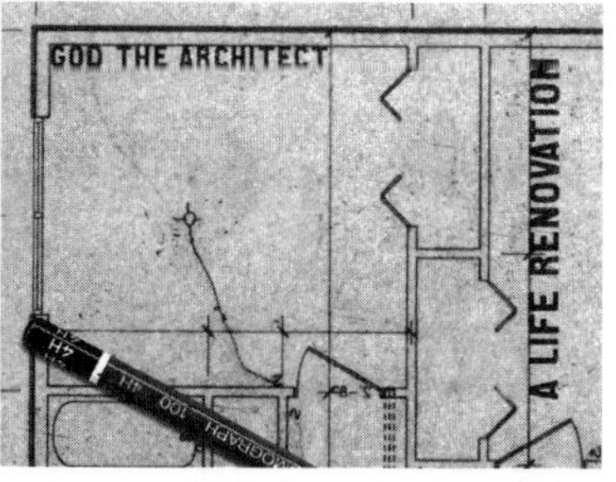

183. ✘ The watchman was found lax *on* his duty.

✔ The watchman was found lax *in* his duty.

184. ✘ One should be honest *with* one's dealings.

✔ One should be honest *in* one's dealings.

185. ✘ You must be temperate *of* your speech.

✔ You must be temperate *in* your speech

186. ✘ This area is backward *at* agriculture.

✔ This area is backward *in* agriculture.

CLUES

The above Adjectives take the preposition *'in'* after them.

187. ✘ She is not acquainted *to* me.

✔ She is not acquainted *with* me.

188. ✘ This house is beset *of* many problems.

✔ This house is beset *with* many problems.

189. ✘ You should be consistent *at* your efforts to attain success.

✔ You should be consistent *with* your efforts to attain success.

190. ✘ The people at the site were overcome *of* grief.

✔ The people at the site were overcome *with* grief.

191. ✘ This saint is endowed *by* divine power.

✔ This saint is endowed *with* divine power.

192. ✘ We must be contented *at* what we have.

✔ We must be contented *with* what we have.

193. ✘ I am fatigued *of* hardwork.

✔ I am fatigued *with* hardwork.

194. ✘ We were drenched *in* rain water.

✔ We were drenched *with* rain water.

195. ✘ You seem to be intimate *of* your neighbour.

✔ You seem to be intimate *with* your neighbour.

196. ✘ Pt. Jahawar Lal Nehru was popular *at* the children.

✔ Pt. Jahawar Lal Nehru was popular *with* the children.

197. ✘ He is not conversant *in* the syllabus of CBSE.

✔ He is not conversant *with* the syllabus of CBSE.

198. ✘ The Director is satisfied *at* my work.

✔ The Director is satisfied *with* my work.

199. ✘ The life of this person is replete *of* many difficulties.

✔ The life of this person is replete *with* many difficulties.

200. ✘ This minister is popular *among* the masses.

✔ This minister is popular *with* the masses.

201. ✘ We are disgusted *at* this servant.

✔ We are disgusted *with* this servant.

202. ✘ We were all delighted *by* the scenic beauty of the hill.

✔ We were all delighted *with* the scenic beauty of the hill.

CLUES

The above Adjectives and Participles take the preposition '*with*' after them.

203. ✘ This man has been accused *for* murder.

✔ This man has been accused *of* murder.

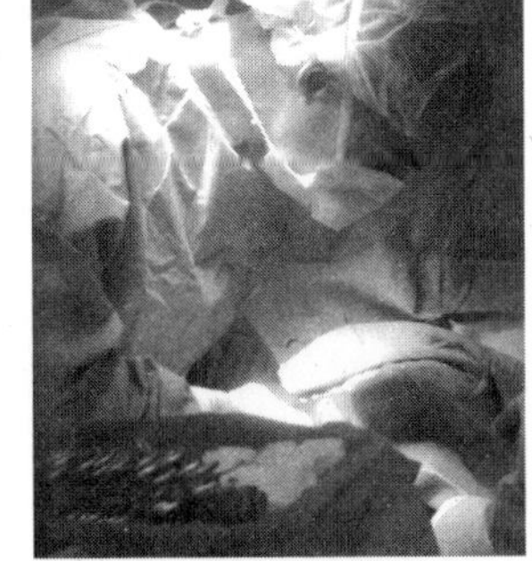

204. ✘ We should not be afraid *from* death.

✔ We should not be afraid *of* death.

205. ✘ The surgeon is apprehensive *with* the patient's recovery.

✔ The surgeon is apprehensive *of* the patient's recovery.

206. ✘ You have been acquitted *in* the allegation.

✔ You have been acquitted *of* the allegation.

207. ✘ I shall apprise you *on* my problems.

✔ I shall apprise you *of* my problems.

208. ✘ The institute has assured you *with* your admission.

✔ The institute has assured you *of* your admission.

209. ✘ He is not aware *with* my health.

✔ He is not aware *of* my health.

210. ✘ He is bereft *from* eye sight.

✔ He is bereft *of* eye sight.

211. ✘ Be cautious *from* the pick-pockets.

✔ Be cautious *of* the pick-pockets.

212. ✘ You should be confident *at* your success.

✔ You should be confident *of* your success.

213. ✘ He is certain *at* his success.

✔ He is certain *of* his success.

214. ✘ I am conscious *in* your financial difficulties.

✔ I am conscious *of* your financial difficulties.

215. ✘ I am confident *at* my success.

✔ I am confident *of* my success.

216. ✘ You should not be deprived *from* your fundamental rights.

✔ You should not be deprived *of* your fundamental rights.

217. ✘ He has been defrauded *with* his belongings.

✔ He has been defrauded *of* his belongings.

218. ✘ My friend is desirous *at* entering civil services.

✔ My friend is desirous *of* entering civil services.

219. ✘ You should not be distrustful *with* your friends.

✔ You should not be distrustful *of* your friends.

220. ✘ Don't be fearful *from* death.

✔ Don't be fearful *of* death.

221. ✘ Every one will receive an award irrespective *at* his performance.

✔ Every one will receive an award irrespective *of* his performance.

222. ✘ John is proud *at* his colleagues.

✔ John is proud *of* his colleagues.

223. ✘ One should be sensible *to* others' feelings.

✔ One should be sensible *of* others' feelings

224. ✘ Be tolerant *at* others if you want to lead a happy life.

✔ Be tolerant *of* others if you want to lead a happy life.

225. ✘ He is worthy *at* being admitted in our institution.

✔ He is worthy *of* being admitted in our institution.

226. ✘ This place is void *in* peace of mind.

✔ This place is void *of* peace of mind.

227. ✘ Don't be vain *at* your strength.

✔ Don't be vain *of* your strength.

228. ✘ He is envious *in* his colleague.

✔ He is envious *of* his colleague.

229. ✘ I am sick *at* this fellow.

✔ I am sick of this fellow.

230. ✘ You seem to be suspicious *at* your friends.

✔ You seem to be suspicious *of* your friends.

231. ✘ Most men are fearful *at* death.

✔ Most men are fearful *of* death.

232. ✘ He is guilty *at* fraud.

✔ He is guilty *of* fraud.

CLUES

The above Adjectives and Participles take the preposition *'of'* after them.

233. ✗ You are not eligible *of* admission.
 ✔ You are not eligible *for* admission.
234. ✗ This person is notorious *at* smuggling.
 ✔ This person is notorious *for* smuggling.

235. ✗ She is good *at* nothing.
 ✔ She is good *for* nothing.
236. ✗ He feels sorry *at* his behaviour.
 ✔ He feels sorry *for* his behaviour.
237. ✗ This medicine is useful *to* the children.
 ✔ This medicine is useful *for* the children.
238. ✗ It is customary *with* us to celebrate this festival.
 ✔ It is customary *for* us to celebrate this festival.
239. ✗ This boy is fit *at* this job.
 ✔ This boy is fit *for* this job.
240. ✗ I am grateful *at* his kindness.
 ✔ I am grateful *for* his kindness.
241. ✗ I am prepared *with* any eventuality.
 ✔ I am prepared *for* any eventuality.
242. ✗ This food is not sufficient *to* them.
 ✔ This food is not sufficient *for* them.

243. ✗ Are you ready *at* the travel?
 ✔ Are you ready *for* the travel?
244. ✗ This ship is destined *to* Iraq.
 ✔ This ship is destined *for* Iraq.

CLUES

The above Adjectives and Participles take the Preposition 'for' after them.

245. ✗ He did not accede *with* our advice.
     ✔ He did not accede *to* our advice.

246. ✗ You have to adapt *at* this surrounding.
     ✔ You have to adapt *to* this surrounding.

247. ✗ You must adhere *with* my advice.
     ✔ You must adhere *to* my advice.

248. ✗ This house is allotted *for* Mr. Rahim.
     ✔ This house is allotted *to* Mr. Rahim.

249. ✗ You should apologize *at* your teacher for your behaviour.
     ✔ You should apologize *to* your teacher for your behaviour.

250. ✗ His delay is ascribed *for* traffic jam.
     ✔ His delay is ascribed *to* traffic jam.

251. ✗ We must aspire *for* noble objectives.
     ✔ We must aspire *after* noble objectives.

252. ✗ I will contribute something *for* public welfare.
     ✔ I will contribute something *to* public welfare.

253. ✘ The nurse is attending *at* the patients.

✔ The nurse is attending *to* the patients.

254. ✘ Your failure is attributed *with* lack of hard work.

✔ Your failure is attributed *to* lack of hard work.

255. ✘ This property belongs *for* Sindhias.

✔ This property belongs *to* Sindhias.

256. ✘ This product does not conform *with* the sample provided to us.

✔ This product does not conform *to* the sample provided to us.

257. ✘ The principal did not consent *with* the teachers' proposal.

✔ The principal did not consent *to* the teachers' proposal.

258. ✘ Some people prefer tea *than* milk.

✔ Some people prefer tea *to* milk.

259. ✘ You should listen *at* the teacher.

✔ You should listen *to* the teacher.

260. ✘ Many patients succumbed *for* the injuries.

✔ Many patients succumbed *to* the injuries.

261. ✘ The soldiers did not yield *with* pressure.

✔ The soldiers did not yield *to* pressure.

262. ✘ They objected *at* our proposal.

✔ They objected *to* our proposal.

CLUES

The above Verbs take the preposition *'to'* after them.

263. ✘ The doctor advised me to abstain *off* alcohol.

✔ The doctor advised me to abstain *from* alcohol.

264. ✘ People are debarred *at* entering this building.

✔ People are debarred *from* entering this building.

265. ✗ The guests alighted *at* the aeroplane.

✔ The guests alighted *from* the aeroplane.

266. ✗ You can derive great benefit *with* this book.

✔ You can derive great benefit *from* this book.

267. ✗ A fairy emerged *out* somewhere.

✔ A fairy emerged *from* somewhere.

268. ✗ He has recovered *with* sickness.

✔ He has recovered *from* sickness.

269. ✗ You should protect this herb *off* extreme heat.

✔ You should protect this herb *from* extreme heat.

270. ✗ People are prohibited *at* entering this house.

✔ People are prohibited *from* entering this house.

271. ✗ You can exclude me *on* the list.

✔ You can exclude me *from* the list.

272. ✗ One must refrain oneself *at* bad habits.

✔ One must refrain oneself *from* bad habits.

CLUES

The above Verbs take the preposition *'from'* after them.

273. ✗ Don't associate *to* bad persons.

✔ Don't associate *with* bad persons.

274. ✗ Kindly bear *to* me in this hour of difficulty.

✔ Kindly bear *with* me in this hour of difficulty.

275. ✗ The party workers clashed *at* their opponents.

✔ The party workers clased *with* their opponents.

276. ✗ I can't cope *up* this work.

✓ I can't cope *with* this work.

277. ✗ The date of his marriage coincided *at* the university examination.

✓ The date of his marriage coincided *with* the university examination.

278. ✗ I disagree *on* him in this matter.

✓ I disagree *with* him on this matter.

279. ✗ All tried to grapple *at* the problem.

✓ All tried to grapple *with* the problem.

280. ✗ Fill this glass *in* water.

✓ Fill this glass *with* water.

281. ✗ Don't meddle *in* his personal affairs.

✓ Don't meddle *with* his personal affairs.

282. ✗ He didn't want to part *from* his pen.

✓ He didn't want to part *with* his pen.

283. ✗ Both the businessmen are vying *at* each other to increase their sale.

✓ Both the businessmen are vying *with* each other to increase their sale.

284. ✗ He quarrelled *at* his neighbours.

✓ He quarrelled *with* his neighbours.

285. ✗ We must sympathize *at* the poor and the downtrodden.

✓ We must sympathize *with* the poor and the downtrodden.

CLUES

The above Verbs take the preposition '*with*' after them.

286. ✗ He has been acquitted *with* the allegation.

✔ He has been acquitted *of* the allegation.

287. ✘ Beware *from* dogs.

✔ Beware *of* dogs.

288. ✘ Don't boast *at* your physical strength. It is short-lived.

✔ Don't boast *of* your physical strength. It is short-lived.

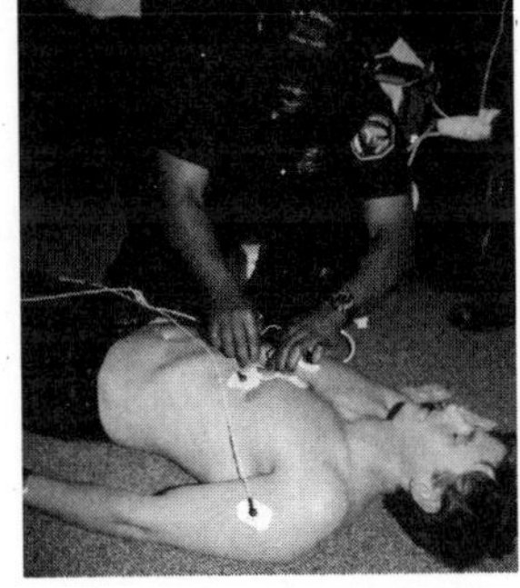

289. ✘ The patient complained *with* chest pain.

✔ The patient complained *of* chest pain.

290. ✘ He dreams *at* becoming a millionaire.

✔ He dreams *of* becoming a millionaire.

291. ✘ Many people died *from* malaria.

✔ Many people died *of* malaria.

292. ✘ The Director has disapproved *at* your proposal.

✔ The Director has disapproved *of* your proposal.

293. ✘ I want to dispose *off* these items.

✔ I want to dispose *of* these items.

294. ✘ He was divested *off* his degree and portfolio.

✔ He was divested *of* his degree and portfolio.

CLUES

The above Verbs take the preposition *'of'* after them.

295. ✘ We must atone *with* our sins.

✔ We must atone *for* our sins.

296. ✘ They are canvassing *to* the Congress candidate.

✔ They are canvassing *for* the Congress candidate.

297. ✘ You must care *of* your aged parents.

✔ You must care *for* your aged parents.

298. ✗ We should hope *at* the best.

✔ We should hope *for* the best.

299. ✗ The doctor is feeling at her pulse.

✔ The doctor is feeling *for* her pulse.

300. ✗ All pine *of* the lost days of one's life.

✔ All pine *for* the lost days of one's life.

301. ✗ Let us start *at* our destination.

✔ Let us start *for* our destination.

302. ✗ He is yearning *at* his old happy days.

✔ He is yearning *for* his old happy days.

CLUES

The above Verbs take the preposition 'for' with them.

303. ✗ He has excelled himself *at* sports.

✔ He has excelled himself *in* sports.

304. ✗ Don't indulge *at* bad habits.

✔ Don't indulge *in* bad habits.

305. ✗ We should persevere *with* difficult times.

✔ We should persevere *in* difficult times.

306. ✗ You should take delight *at* this scenery.

✔ You should take delight *in* this scenery.

CLUES

The above Verbs take the preposition *'in'* after them.

307. ✗ You should decide *at* your future course of action.

✔ You should decide *on* your future course of action.

308. ✗ I didn't comment *at* your answer.

✔ I didn't comment *on* your answer.

309. ✗ Don't encroach *with* this property.

✔ Don't encroach *on* this property.

310. ✘ Success depends *at* hardwork.

✔ Success depends *on* hardwork.

311. ✘ He tries to impose his decision *at* others.

✔ He tries to impose his decision *on* others.

312. ✘ You should insist *at* getting your salary in time.

✔ You should insist *on* getting your salary in time.

CLUES

The above Verbs take the preposition *'on'* after them.

11

Handling Paronyms

A word which is similar in form of derivation but different in meaning is known as Paronym. Like homonyms, paronyms also perplex the students a lot as they erroneously use one for another, as they do not know the exact meaning of the parts.

Below is given a list of confusing paronyms.

1. ✘ Many refugees are living in *object* poverty.
   ✔ Many refugees are living in *abject* poverty.
2. ✘ His main *abject* in life is to become a pilot.
   ✔ His main *object* in life is to become a pilot.
3. ✘ The employees were *aloud* to go on leave.
   ✔ The employees were *allowed* to go on leave.
4. ✘ Don't speak *loud.*
   ✔ Don't speak *aloud.*
5. ✘ My house is *adjoining* to a stadium.
   ✔ My house is *adjacent* to a stadium.
6. ✘ The cinema theatre *adjacents* the post office.
   ✔ The cinema theatre *adjoins* the post office.
7. ✘ He could not get *admission* to chairman's office.
   ✔ He could not get *admittance* to chairman's office.

8. ✘ He got *admittance* into the college of his choice.

✔ He got *admission* into the college of his choice.

9. ✘ The day is *alternative* by night.

✔ The day is *alternated* by night.

10. ✘ There is no *alternated* to hardwork.

✔ There is no *alternative* to hardwork.

11. ✘ I am interested in *antiquated* English literature.

✔ I am interested in *ancient* English literature.

12. ✘ The Aryans are *ancient* people.

✔ The Aryans are *antiquated* people.

13. ✘ Johnson is a popular film *artist.*

✔ Johnson is a popular film *artiste.*

14. ✘ You seem to be a great *artiste.*

✔ You seem to be a great *artist.*

15. ✘ My friend is an experienced *artist.*

✔ My friend is an experienced *artisan.*

CLUES

(i) A word which is similar in form of derivation but different in meaning is known as a paronym.

(i) Abject - hopeless

(ii) Object -aim

(iii) Allowed - gave permission

(iv) aloud - in a loud voice

(v) Adjacent - lying near

(vi) Adjoining - next

(vii) Admittance - being admitted to a place

(viii) Admission - being admitted into an academic institution

(ix) Alternate - one after another

(x) Alternative - the other choice of the two

(xi) Ancient - old in time

(xii) Antiquated - old in fashion

(xiii) Artist - an expert in fine arts

(xiv) Artiste - an actor by profession

(xv) Artisan - a person who practises some handicrafts

16. ✘ This medicine is *beneficient* to health.

    ✔ This medicine is *beneficial* to health.

17. ✘ She is a *beneficial* woman.

    ✔ She is a *beneficent* woman.

18. ✘ She has a *childish* face.

    ✔ She has a *childlike* face.

19. ✘ I was fed up with his *child like* behaviour.

    ✔ I was fed up with his *childish* behaviour.

20. ✘ The principal gave *clearness* to the proposal.

    ✔ The principal gave *clearance* to the proposal.

21. ✘ There is no *clearance* in your essay.

    ✔ There is no *clearness* in your essay.

22. ✘ He is *confidant* of getting distinction in all the subjects.

    ✔ He is *confident* of getting distinction in all the subjects.

23. ✘ The *continual* hardwork will tell upon your health.

    ✔ The *continuous* hardwork will tell upon your health.

24. ✘ The *continuous* torrential rain overflooded the town.

    ✔ The *continual* torrential rain overflooded the town.

25. ✘ *Corporeal* punishment has been abolished by many countries.

✔ *Corporal* punishment has been abolished by many countries.

26. ✘ I have no *confident* in my life.

✔ I have no *confidant* in my life.

27. ✘ One should not run after *corporal* pleasures.

✔ One should not run after *corporeal* pleasures.

28. ✘ Fiction is an *imaginative* story.

✔ Fiction is an *imaginary* story.

29. ✘ Shakespeare was an *imaginary* writer.

✔ Shakespeare was an *imaginative* writer.

30. ✘ He is an *industrial* boy.

✔ He is an *industrious* boy.

31. ✘ Noida is an industrious town.

✔ Noida is an industrial town.

CLUES

(i) Beneficial - useful

(ii) Beneficent kind

(iii) Childlike - simple and innocent

(iv) Childish - foolish

(v) Clearance - permission

(vi) Clearness - clarity

(vii) Confident - having a feeling of confidence

(viii) Confidant - a person who is trusted with private affairs

(ix) Continuous - uninterrupted in a particular action

(x) Continual - without intermission

(xi) Corporal - physical

(xii) Cosporeal - tangible

(xiiii) Imaginary - unreal

(xiv) Imaginative - creative

(xv) Industrial - relating to industry

(xvi) Industrious - hardworking.

32. ✘ The accused was kept in a *judicious* custody.

    ✔ The accused was kept in a *judicial* custody.

33. ✘ You should take a *judicial* decision.

    ✔ You should take a *judicious* decision.

34. ✘ Every one has some *memorial* incidents in his life.

    ✔ Every one has some *memorable* incidents in his life.

35. ✘ A *memorable* shall be erected at this place.

    ✔ A *memorial* shall be erected at this place.

36. ✘ We should not hurt the feelings of *sensible* persons.

    ✔ We should not hurt the feelings of *sensitive* persons.

37. ✘ He took a *sensitive* decision.

    ✔ He took a *sensible* decision.

38. ✘ Mrs. Bharti is a *social* woman.

    ✔ Mrs. Bharti is a *sociable* woman.

39. ✘ We should endeavour to eradicate *sociable* problems.

    ✔ Who should endeavour to eradicate *social* problems.

40. ✘ Shakespeare was a *populous* playwright.

✔ Shakespeare was a *popular* playwright.

41. ✘ Kolkata is a *popular* city.

✔ Kolkata is a *populous* city.

42. ✘ Every one likes the *amicable* qualities in others.

✔ Every one likes the *amiable* qualities in others.

43. ✘ You should find an *amiable* solution to the problem.

✔ You should find an *amicable* solution to the problem.

44. ✘ I don't like *artificial* persons.

✔ I don't like *artful* persons.

45. ✘ The readers were not impressed with the *artful* language of the author.

✔ The readers were not impressed with the artificial language of the author.

46. ✘ Shyam Banegal is an *artful* film director.

✔ Shyam Banegal is an *artistic* film director.

47. ✘ He sat *besides* his father.

✔ He sat *beside* his father.

48. ✗ *Beside* owning a scooter he owns a Maruti car.

✔ *Besides* owning a scooter he owns a Maruti car.

49. ✗ The principal delivered a *ceremonial* speech.

✔ The principal delivered a ceremonious speech.

50. ✗ The cadets were wearing *ceremonious* dress.

✔ The cadets were wearing *ceremonial* dress.

51. ✗ I have written a *comprehensible* English grammar.

✔ I have written a *comprehensive* English grammar.

52. ✗ The language used in this book is not *comprehensive.*

✔ The language used in this book is not *comprehensible.*

CLUES

(i) Judicial - relating to justice

(ii) Judicious - prudent

(iii) Memorable - worthy of being remembered

(iv) Memorial - a symbol or statue or building erected to remind people of an event or a person

(v) Sensitive - emotional

(vi) Sensible - reasonable

(vii) Sociable - friendly

(viii) Social - relating to society

(ix) Popular - famous

(x) Populous - crowded

(xi) amiable - lovable

(xii) Amicable - friendly

(xiii) Artful - cunning or clever

(xiv) Artificial - unnatural

(xiv) Artistic - having aesthetic qualities

(xvi) Beside - By the side of

(xvii) Besides - In addition to (or) apart from

(xviii) Ceremonious - observing formalities

(xix) Ceremonial - associated with ceremony

(xx) Comprehensive - exhaustive

(xxi) Comprehensible - understandable.

53. ✘ Our *destiny* is far off and it is already dark.

✔ Our *destination* is far off and it is already dark.

54. ✘ The *destination* of all beings is in the hands of the Almighty.

✔ The *destiny* of all beings is in the hands of the Almighty.

55. ✘ The *estimation* of the project is yet to be finalised.

✔ The *estimate* of the project is yet to be finalised.

56. ✘ According to my *estimate,* we should start now.

✔ According to my *estimation,* we should start now.

57. ✘ We all must have *estimation* for the elders.

✔ We all must have *esteem* for the elders.

58. ✘ Many people want to lead a *luxuriant* life.

✔ Many people want to lead a *luxurious* life.

59. ✘ There is a *luxurious* growth around this bungalow.

✔ There is a *luxuriant* growth around this bungalow.

60. ✘ Life can give only *momentous* pleasures.

✔ Life can give only *momentary* pleasures.

61. ✘ He is on *officious* tour.

✔ He is on *official* tour.

62. ✘ Some people are *official* by nature.

✔ Some people are *officious* by nature.

63. ✘ Your *acceptation* of my invitation shall be a great pleasure to me.

✔ Your *acceptance* of my invitation shall be a great pleasure to me.

64. ✘ I don't know the *acceptance* of this word.

✔ I don't know the *acceptation* of this word.

65. ✘ Some *barbarity* is still prevalent in some parts of the world.

✔ Some *barbarism* is still prevalent in some parts of the world.

66. ✘ The cruel dictator was notorious for his *barabarism.*

67. ✔ The cruel dictator was notorious for his *barbarity.*

68. ✘ No one can achieve *completion* in any field.

✔ No one can achieve *completeness* in any field.

69. ✘ *Completeness* of an arduous task gives us joy.

✔ *Completion* of an arduous task gives us joy.

CLUES

(i) Destination - goal

(ii) Destiny - fate

(iii) Estimate - calculation

(iv) Estimation - opinion

(v) Esteem - respect

(vi) Luxurious - full of luxury or comfortable

(vii) Luxuriant - rich in growth

(viii) Momentary - temporary

(ix) Momentous - very important, significant

(x) Official - pertaining to an office

(xi) Officious - eager to offer service or help

(xii) Acceptance - on act of accepting something

(xiii) Acceptation - meaning

(xiv) Barbarism - uncivilised conditions

(xv) Barbarity - cruelty

(xvi) Completeness - Perfection

(xvii) Completion - the act of ending or finishing.

70. ✘ His behaviour was *contemptuous.*

    ✔ His behaviour was *contemptible.*

71. ✘ I am *comtemptible* of my friend's insincerity.

    ✔ I am *comtemptuous* of my friend's insincerity

72. ✘ There is a *considerate* improvement in his health.

    ✔ There is a *considerable* improvement in his health.

73. ✘ *Dependency* on others may lead to exploitation.

    ✔ *Dependence* on others may lead to exploitation.

74. ✘ Our country was a *dependence* of the U.K.

    ✔ Our country was a *dependency* of the U.K.

75. ✘ He, being an *uninterested* person, is liked by all.

    ✔ He, being an *disinterested* person, is liked by all.

76. ✘ He is *disinterested* in science.

    ✔ He is *uninterested* in science.

77. ✘ He got *distinctness* in English.

    ✔ He got *distinction* in English.

78. ✘ There is no *distinction* in your writing.

    ✔ There is no *distinctness* in your writing.

79. ✘ We want to get *delivery* from this servant.

✔ We want to get *deliverance* from this servant.

80. ✘ The *deliverance* of the principal's speech was excellent.

✔ The *delivery* of the principal's speech was excellent.

81. ✘ We must find out a *devise* to improve the management.

✔ We must find out a *device* to improve the management.

82. ✘ He *devices* new methods to cheat others.

✔ He *devises* new methods to cheat others.

CLUES

(i) Contemptible - deserving contempt

(ii) Comtemptuous - hateful

(iii) Considerable - moderately large

(iv) Considerate - thoughtful

(v) Dependence - reliance

(vi) Dependency - a subject country

(vii) Disinterested - unselfish

(viii) Uninterested - having no interest

(ix) Distinctness - clarity

(x) Distinction - honour

(xi) Deliverance - Freedom

(xii) Delivery - (i) the way of expression
(ii) giving of the letter
(iii) giving birth to a child

(xiii) Device (Noun) method

(xiv) Devise (verb) invent

83. ✘ She has an *envious* personality.

✔ She has an *enviable* personality.

84. ✗ You should not be *enviable* of others' progress.

✔ You should not be *envious* of others' progress.

85. ✗ His method of teaching is *effectual.*

✔ His method of teaching is *effective.*

86. ✗ You did not make *effective* statement.

✔ You did not make *effectual* statement.

87. ✗ This herb will prove *effectual* in controlling your blood pressure.

✔ This herb will prove *efficacious* in controlling your blood pressure.

89. ✗ My friend is an *egoist* because he always talks about himself.

✔ My friend is an *egotist* because he always talks about himself.

90. ✗ A person who is interested in his self is called *egotist.*

✔ A person who is interested in his self is called *egoist.*

91. ✗ Man has tried to control *elementary* powers.

✔ Man has tried to control *elemental* powers.

92. ✗ You must have an *elemental* knowledge of English grammar.

✔ You must have an *elementary* knowledge of English grammar.

93. ✗ After the ship-wreck, many passengers died of *exposition.*

✔ After the ship-wreck, many passengers died of *exposure.*

94. ✗ Your *exposure* of the illiteracy problems in India was not satisfactory.

✔ Your *exposition* of the illiteracy problems in India was not satisfactory.

95. ✗ The leaders of our country should try to improve the *economical* conditions of the country.

✔ The leaders of our country should try to improve the *economic* conditions of the country.

96. ✗ Wise people live *economic* life.

✔ Wise people live *economical* life.

97. ✗ Many people were present at the *funereal* ceremony of my grandfather.

✔ Many people were present at the *funeral* ceremony of my grandfather.

98. ✗ Why are you looking *funeral* today?

✔ Why are you looking *funereal* today?

CLUES

1. Enviable - that can be envied.
2. Envious - feeling envy.
3. Effective - powerful.
4. Effectual - having the desired effect.
5. Efficacious - sure to have expected result.
6. Egotist - A person who talks about himself.
7. Egoist - A person who is interested in himself.
8. Elemental - pertaining to elements.
9. Elementary - rudimentary.
10. Exposure - being exposed to air and cold.
11. Exposition - Explanation.
12. Economic - relating to economics
13. Economical - inexpensive.
14. Funeral - burial procession or ceremony.
15. Funereal - gloomy.

99. ✘ Some people do not like *formality* in religion.

✔ Some people do not like *formalism* in religion.

100. ✘ There is official *formalism* to be adhered to in administration.

✔ There is official *formality* to be adhered to in administration.

101. ✘ Many people died in the *fateful* accident.

✔ Many people died in the *fatal* accident.

102. ✘ Republic Day is a *fatal* day for our country.

✔ Republic Day is a fateful day for our country.

103. ✘ Some persons are *fateful* by nature.

✔ Some persons are *fatalist* for nature.

104. ✘ Children wear *festive* dresses on their birthday.

✔ Children wear *festal* dresses on their birthday.

105. ✘ He is in a *festal* mood today.

✔ He is in a *festive* mood today.

106. ✘ She put forward *forcible* arguments.

✔ She put forward *forceful* arguments.

107. ✘ The thieves made *forceful* entry into the house.

✔ The thieves made *forcible* entry into the house.

108. ✘ He is the *hounourable* member of the group housing society.

✔ He is the *honorary* member of the group housing society.

109. ✘ Mother Teresa was an *honorary* woman.

✔ Mother Teresa was an *honourable* woman.

110. ✘ We visited *historic* places in Bangladesh.

✔ We visited historical places in Bangladesh.

111. ✗ Attaining independence from the British rule was a *historical* moment for India.

✔ Attaining independence from the British rule was a *historic* moment for India.

112. ✗ He is an *intelligible* person.

✔ He is an *intelligent* person.

113. ✗ Your handwriting is not *intelligent.*

✔ Your handwriting is not *intelligible.*

114. ✗ There is no *limitation* to knowledge.

✔ There is no *limit* to knowledge.

115. ✗ There is a *limit* to the success of this project.

✔ There is a *limitation* to the success of this project.

CLUES

(i) Formalism - habitual observance of rules

(ii) Formality - ceremony, show

(iii) Fatal - that ends in death

(iv) Fateful - important

(v) Fatalist - A person who believes in fate

(vi) Festal - pertaining to a festival or feast

(vii) Festive - happy, joyous

(viii) Forceful - effective

(ix) Forcible - by force

(x) Honorary - an office without remuneration

(xi) Honourable - worthy of honour

(xii) Historic - important

(xiii) Historical - pertaining to history

(xiv) Intelligent - wise

(xv) Intelligible - understandable

(xvi) Limit - boundary.

(xvii) Limitation-restriction or obstacle

116. ✘ A doctor must keep with him the medical *necessaries.*

✔ A doctor must keep with him the medical *necessities.*

117. ✘ My employer promised that he would provide me with the *necessities.*

✔ My employer promised that he would provide me with the *necessaries.*

118. ✘ He is *neglectful* in his studies.

✔ He is *negligent* in his studies.

119. ✘ He is *negligent* of posting the letter.

✔ He is *neglectful* of posting the letter.

120. ✘ He has made *neglectful* improvement in his studies.

✔ He has made *negligible* improvement in his studies.

121. ✘ The *observation* of discipline leads to success.

✔ The *observance* of discipline leads to success.

122. ✘ He has keen *observance* of the people of tribal India.

✔ He has keen *observation* of the people of tribal India.

123. ✘ Many people are not *practicable* towards life.

✔ Many people are not *practical* towards life.

124. ✘ Your proposals are not *practical.*

✔ Your proposals are not *practicable.*

125. ✘ All took sympathy on his *pitiful* condition.

✔ All took sympathy on his *pitiable* condition.

126. ✘ He was *pitiable* at his friend's death.

✔ He was *pitiful* at his friend's death.

127. ✘ We heard the *pitiable* cries of the patients in the hospital.

✔ We heard the *piteous* cries of the patients in the hospital.

128. ✘ His *porphesy* of the rain came true.

✔ His *prophecy* of the rain came true.

129. ✘ The weather office will *prophecy* that there will be rains next month.

✔ The weather office will *prophesy* that there will be rains next month.

130. ✘ He has done many *respectful* deeds.

✔ He has done many *respectable* deeds.

131. ✘ All the people present were *respectable* to the principal.

✔ All the people present were respectful to the principal.

132. ✘ All were requested to be seated in their *respectful* chairs.

✔ All were requested to be seated in their *respective* chairs.

133. ✘ The *rightful* persons have bright future.

✔ The *righteous* persons have bright future.

134. ✘ He was *regretable* at his friend's death.

✔ He was *regretful* at his friend's death.

135. ✘ It is *regretful* that you have not fared well in the examination.

✔ It is *regretable* that you have not fared well in the examination.

136. ✘ Wise persons do not run after *sensuous* pleasures.

✔ Wise persons do not run after *sensual* pleasures.

137. ✘ William *Wordsworth* was a *sensual* poet.

✔ William *Wordsworth* was a *sensuous* poet.

CLUES

(i) Necessaries - essential things

(ii) Necessities - urgent needs

(iii) Negligent - careless in duties or things

(iv) Neglectful - careless as a matter of habit

(v) Negligible - that can be ignored

(vi) Observance - practice

(vii) Observation - the power of keenness

(viii) Practical - realistic

(ix) Practicable - capable of being practised

(x) Pitiable - arousing pity

(xi) Pitiful - feeling pity

(xii) Piteous - full of pity, sad

(xiii) Prophecy (Noun) - a forecast or prediction

(xiv) Prophesy (verb) - to make a forecast

(xv) Respectable - deserving respect

(xvi) Respectful - showing respect

(xvii) Respective - particular or specific

(xviii) Righteous - just

(xix) Rightful - having a just and legal claim

(xx) Regretful - full of regret and sadness.

(xxi) Regrettable - causing regret.

(xxii) Sensual - depending on the senses and not on the spirit.

(xxiii) Sensuous - affecting the senses especially aesthetically.

138. ✘ We should not underestimate the *signification* of female education.

✔ We should not underestimate the *significance* of female education.

139. ✘ He does not understand the *significance* of many difficult words.

✔ He does not understand the *signification* of many difficult words.

140. ✘ Gandhi ji attached much importance to *spirituous* education.

✔ Gandhi ji attached much importance to *spiritual* education.

141. ✘ *Spiritual* drinks are injurious to health.

✔ *Spirituous* drinks are injurious to health.

142. ✘ Your behaviour is not *tolerant.*

✔ Your behaviour is not *tolerable.*

143. ✘ We should be *tolerable* of all religions.

✔ We should be *tolerant* of all religions.

144. ✘ One should exercise *temperament* in alcoholic drinks.

✔ One should exercise *temperance* in alcoholic drinks.

145. ✘ Health, wealth and life are *temporal.*

✔ Health, wealth and life are *temporary.*

146. ✘ We should not run after *temporary* pleasures.

✔ We should not run after *temporal* pleasures.

147. ✘ Most of the politicians are considered to be *immoral.*

✔ Most of the politicians are considered to be *unmoral.*

148. ✘ One should not indulge in *unmoral* activities.

✔ One should not indulge in *immoral* activities.

149. ✘ *Unison* is strength.

✔ *Union* is strength.

150. ✘ National anthem was sung in *union.*

✔ National anthem was sung in *unison.*

151. ✘ There is *unison* in diversity in our country.

✔ There is *unity* in diversity in our country.

152. ✘ The king is the *virtuous* dictator of this country.

✔ The king is the *virtual* dictator of this country.

CLUES

(i) Signification - meaning

(ii) Significance - importance

(iii) Spiritual - pertaining to soul or spirit

(iv) Spirituous - alcoholic

(v) Tolerable - which can be tolerated

(vi) Tolerant - having tolerance

(vii) Temperance - having moderation

(viii) Temperament - disposition

(ix) Temporary - short-lived

(x) Temporal - physical

(xi) Unmoral - having no regard for morals

(xii) Immoral - dishonest

(xiii) Union - act of uniting

(xiv) Unison - agreement of sounds or voices

(xv) Unity - Oneness

(xvi) Virtual - real

(xvii) Virtuous - righteous, blameless.

153. ✘ She is *wilful* to work hard.

✔ She is *willing* to work hard.

154. ✘ His involvement in the crime was *willing*.

✔ His involvement in the crime was *wilful*.

155. ✘ I could not *await* for him.

✔ I could not *wait* for him.

156. ✘ She was *waiting* the results.

✔ She was *awaiting* the results.

157. ✘ She is liked by all for having *womanish* love and affection.

✔ She is liked by all for having *womanly* love and affection.

158. ✗ No one likes him for his *womanly* habits.

✓ No one likes him for his *womanish* habits.

159. ✗ What is your *vacation*?

✓ What is your *vocation*?

160. ✗ His *vocation* is gardening.

✓ His *avocation* is gardening.

161. ✗ He wants to spend his *avocation* in Shimla.

✓ He wants to spend his *vacation* in Shimla.

162. ✗ What is the *specialty* of her teaching?

✓ What is the *speciality* of her teaching?

163. ✗ Her *specialty* is mountaineering.

✓ Her *speciality* is mountaineering.

164. ✗ It is impossible to live in complete *servility*.

✓ It is impossible to live in complete *servitude*.

165. ✗ The *servitude* of women sometimes proves dangerous to their existence.

✓ The *servility* of women sometimes proves dangerous to their existence.

166. ✗ There is no *proportionate* distribution of wealth in India.

✓ There is no *proportional* distribution of wealth in India.

167. ✗ Your salary is not *proportional* to the hardwork done by you.

✓ Your salary is not *proportionate to* the hardwork done by you.

CLUES

1. Willing - desirous, willing.
2. Wilful - deliberate.
3. Wait - to wait for someone.

4. Await - to wait for something.
5. Womanly - kind and affectionate.
6. Womanish - weak and cowardly.
7. Vocation - chief occupation or profession.
8. Avocation - hobby.
9. Vacation - holidays.
10. Speciality - striking quality.
11. Specialty - specific pursuit or skill.
12. Servitude - the state of slavery.
13. Servility - a sense of servitude.
14. Proportional - in due proportion.
15. Proportionate - equal.

168. ✘ He did not take a *political* decision by resigning his job.

✔ He did not take a *politic* decision by resigning his job.

169. ✘ Science students are generally not interested in *politic* matters.

✔ Science students are generally not interested in *political* matters.

170. ✘ You are *prudential* enough to take right decisions.

✔ You are *prudent* enough to take right decisions.

171. ✘ He appreciated the *prudent* proposals of his nephew.

✔ He appreciated the *prudential* proposals of his nephew.

172. ✘ Some people are *providential* in their thoughts.

✔ Some people are *provident* in their thoughts.

173. ✘ All must submit to provident will.

✔ All must *submit* to providential will.

174. ✘ The Ganges is a *Godlike* river.

✔ The Ganges is a *Godly* river.

175. ✘ Mahatma Gandhi was *a Godly* person.

✔ Mahatma Gandhi was a *Godlike* person.

176. ✘ She has a *special* sympathy for the poor.

✔ She has a *especial* sympathy for the poor.

177. ✘ You should use this medicine in *especial* cases only.

✔ You should use this medicine in *special* cases only.

178. ✘ He has *decisive* opinion that he will resign his job.

✔ He has *decided* opinion that he will resign his job.

179. ✘ The decision of the judge is *decided.*

✔ The decision of the judge is *decisive.*

180. ✘ Diverse members *participated* in the seminar.

✔ Divers members *participated* in the seminar.

181. ✘ He holds *divers* opinion about religion.

✔ He holds *diverse* opinion about religion.

182. ✘ You should not feel *complaisant* on your success and should keep working hard.

✔ You should not feel *complacent* on your success and should keep working hard.

183. ✘ She is a *complacent* woman.

✔ She is a *complaisant* woman.

CLUES

(i) Politic - wise, prudent

(ii) Political - pertaining to politics

(iii) Provident - having foresight

(iv) Providential - divine

(v) Prudent - wise, intelligent

(vi) Prudential - ideas or plans with prudence

(vii) Godly - holy, pious

(viii) Godlike - like God

(ix) Especial - exceptional

(x) Special - specific

(xi) Decided - definite

(xii) Decisive - that settles a matter or controversy

(xiii) Divers - several or sundry

(xiv) Diverse - Markedly different

(xv) Complacent - pleased, well-satisfied

(xvi) Complaisant - polite.

12

Erroneous Letter Writing

Despite the invention and spread of telecommunication, the simple letter, typed or handwritten on paper remains the most popular means of communication for social, cultural, technical, official, administrative and commercial purposes.

Although it is a fun to receive letters, yet all the letters are not penned so as to look well-written and persuasive. Many errors are committed while we write letters. Inaccurate and erroneous correspondence reflects not only carelessness but also lack of seriousness and consideration towards the person addressed. As accuracy should be the hallmark of an effective letter, a small error in writing a letter may create misunderstanding and wrong interpretation .

1. ✘ April 26th, 2006.

   ✔ 26th April, 2006.

2. ✘ 26 April 2006.

   ✔ April 26, 2006.

3. ✘ Mr. Nelson Athorton ESQ.

   ✔ Nelson Athorton ESQ.

4. ✘ Your's faithfully.

   ✔ Yours faithfully.

5. ✘ Yours affectionately friend.
   ✔ Your affectionate friend.
6. ✘ Very affectionate yours.
   ✔ Very affectionately yours.
7. ✘ Yours Truely.
   ✔ Yours truly.
8. ✘ Cordially your.
   ✔ Cordially yours.
9. ✘ Your's obediently.
   ✔ Yours obediently.
10. ✘ Your's sincerely.
   ✔ Yours sincerely.
11. ✘ Greatfully yours.
   ✔ Gratefully yours.
12. ✘ Thank for your letter.
   ✔ Thanks for your letter.
13. ✘ Thanks you.
   ✔ Thanking you.
14. ✘ Accept my heart-felt congratulations.
   ✔ Accept my heartiest congratulations.
15. ✘ Kindly accept my heartiest condolences.
   ✔ Kindly accept my heart-felt condolences.
16. ✘ Kindly reply at once.
   ✔ Kindly reply soon.
17. ✘ May I ask you favour?
   ✔ May I ask you a favour?
18. ✘ Please reply without failing.
   ✔ Please reply without fail.

19. ✘ Promotion in this office means more hardworking.
✔ Promotion in this office means more hardwork.

20. ✘ The best of fate in your new position.
✔ The best of luck in your new position.

21. ✘ This promotion is a step-stone to further rise.
✔ This promotion is a stepping stone to further rise.

22. ✘ This news has made me happy immeasurably.
✔ This news has made me happy beyond measure.

23. ✘ You should come and bless the baby at the quickest.
✔ You should come and bless the baby at the earliest.

24. ✘ My most dearest son.
✔ My dearest son.

25. ✘ Many happy return of the day.
✔ Many happy returns of the day.

26. ✘ I hope that you are all hail and hearty.
✔ I hope that you are all hale and hearty.

27. ✘ With best complements.
✔ With best compliments.

28. ✘ Give my respect to your parents.
✔ Give my respects to your parents.

29. ✘ Please send receipt of the letter.
✔ Please acknowledge the letter.

30. ✘ Please reply earlier.
✔ Please reply at the earliest.

31. ✘ No other pair can ever be better suited to each other.
✔ No other couple can ever be better suited to each other.

32. ✘ I am anxiously awaiting for your reply.
✔ I am anxiously waiting for your reply.

33. ✗ May you experience martial bliss!

✔ May you experience marital bliss!

34. ✗ I don't know how to tell my happiness on this auspicious occasion.

✔ I don't know how to express my happiness on this auspicious occasion.

35. ✗ Many a thanks for your letter.

✔ Many a thank for your letter.

36. ✗ Your greeting on my birthday made me very happy.

✔ Your greetings on my birthday made me very happy.

37. ✗ We are in receipt of your greetings card.

✔ We are in receipt of your greeting card.

38. ✗ I regret too much not to be able to attend your sister's wedding.

✔ I very much regret not to be able to attend your sister's wedding.

39. ✗ I am sorry for not answering your letter earlier.

✔ I am sorry for not replying your letter earlier.

40. ✗ In accordance to your request.

✔ As requested by you.

41. ✗ I own you an apology for causing inconvenience to you.

✔ I owe you an apology for causing inconvenience to you.

42. ✗ We hope to receive your cheque or the reply.

✔ We hope to receive either your cheque or the reply.

43. ✗ I am looking forward to hearing from you soon.

✔ I look forward to hearing from you soon.

44. ✗ We guarantee free and prompt after-sell service.

✔ We guarantee free and prompt after-sales service.

45. ✗ Your parents dropped the other day on their way to church.

✔ Your parents dropped in the other day on their way to church.

46. ✘ So much has happened when I last wrote you.
✔ So much has happened since I last wrote you.

47. ✘ Thanks a millions for your letter.
✔ Thanks a million for your letter.

48. ✘ We are mostly grateful for your prompt reply.
✔ We are most grateful for your prompt reply.

49. ✘ I'll remain debted to you for your timely help.
✔ I'll remain indebted to you for your timely help.

50. ✘ Thank you from the base of my heart.
✔ Thank you from the bottom of my heart.

51. ✘ Warm congratulation on your brilliant success.
✔ Warm congratulations on your brilliant success.

52. ✘ Wishing best of every thing to you.
✔ Wishing the best of every thing to you.

53. ✘ I love you, will always.
✔ I love you, and always will.

54. ✘ We were terrible upset to learn of your serious accident.
✔ We were terribly upset to learn of your serious accident.

55. ✘ Your condolences had have been _ _ _ _ _ _ .
✔ Your condolences have had been _ _ _ _ _ _ .

56. ✘ We are really fortunate to have such a nice friend as you.
✔ We are really fortunate to have such a nice friend like you.

57. ✘ We regret our unability to accept your invitation.
✔ We regret our inability to accept your invitation.

58. ✘ We feel honoured at being invited.
✔ We feel honoured on being invited.

13

Slipshod Idioms and Phrases

Idioms and phrases make language pithy, tense and flowery. They being problematic in their use, one has to be careful as regards to their meanings and spellings. As idioms and phrases are colourful and enliven the whole system of the language as no other device can, one must learn the correct use of these to speak and write English correctly.

1. ✘ The present problems will soon blow *off*.

   ✔ The present problems will soon blow *over*.

2. ✘ She backed *with* her friend's claim.

   ✔ She backed *up* her friend's claim.

3. ✘ The police produced evidence to bear *with* the charge of murder.

   ✔ The police produced evidence to bear *out* the charge of murder.

4. ✘ The matter has been cleared off.
   ✔ The matter has been cleared up.
5. ✘ I am ready to dispose *off* my car for Rs. 80,000.
   ✔ I am ready to dispose *of* my car for Rs. 80,000.
6. ✘ Rust has eaten *up* the plate.
   ✔ Rust has eaten *away* the plate.
7. ✘ The principal fixed *at* him to complete the work.
   ✔ The principal fixed *upon* him to complete the work.
8. ✘ Your good behaviour has gained *at* the principal.
   ✔ Your good behaviour has gained *on* the principal.
9. ✘ The habit of consuming alcohol has been growing *at* the modern youth.
   ✔ The habit of consuming alcohol has been growing *upon* the modern youth. 
10. ✘ You should hear me *with*.
    ✔ You should hear me *out*.
11. ✘ I have hit *at* a good plan.
    ✔ I have hit *upon* a good plan.
12. ✘ I saw a fellow hanging *out* your house.
    ✔ I saw a fellow hanging *about* your house.
13. ✘ Such events led up *at* the establishment of a democratic government.
    ✔ Such events led *up to* the establishment of a democratic government.
14. ✘ I can not prevail *at* him to attend the function.
    ✔ I can not prevail *on* him to attend the function.
15. ✘ You should try to shake *of* your shyness.
    ✔ You should try to shake *off* your shyness.

16. ✗ Let us stick out *at* better terms.

✓ Let us stick out *for* better terms.

17. ✗ You have trumped *with* a story.

✓ You have trumped *up* a story.

18. ✗ My son bore *at* many prizes at the school sports.

✓ My son bore *away* many prizes at the school sports.

19. ✗ God gives us strength to bear *with* in our adversity.

✓ God gives us strength to bear *up* in our adversity.

20. ✗ I hope you will bear *at* me for a few minutes more.

✓ I hope you will bear *with* me for a few minutes more.

21. ✗ The burglars broke *at* the house.

✓ The burglars broke *into* the house.

22. ✗ The publishers have brought at a new edition of this book.

✓ The publishers have brought out a new edition of this book.

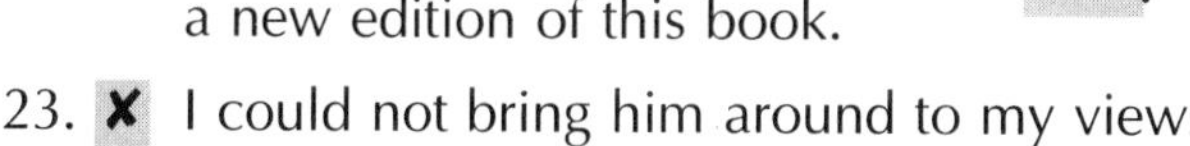

23. ✗ I could not bring him around to my views.

✓ I could not bring him round to my views.

24. ✗ The principal will call *at* an explanation of your conduct.

✓ The principal will call *for* an explanation of your conduct.

25. ✗ Call *for* a doctor immediately.

✓ Call in a doctor immediately.

26. ✗ Can you call us at tomorrow?

✓ Can you call us on tomorrow?

27. ✗ Are you able to call *with* past events?

✓ Are you able to call *up* past events?

28. ✘ The soldiers carried *on* the order of the captain.

✔ The soldiers carried *out* the order of the captain.

29. ✘ My son will carry *out* my business in my absence.

✔ My son will carry *on* my business in my absence.

30. ✘ Many persons have been carried *of* by AIDS.

✔ Many persons have been carried *off* by AIDS.

31. ✘ How did such things come *at*?

✔ How did such things come *about*?

32. ✘ How did you come *with* this book?

✔ How did you come *by* this book?

33. ✘ The question will come *at* before the Municipal Corporation next week.

✔ The question will come *up* before the Municipal Corporation next week.

34. ✘ All cried out *with* such injustice.

✔ All cried out *against* such injustice.

35. ✘ She was cut *of* in the prime of her life.

✔ She was cut *off* in the prime of her life.

36. ✘ We must cut *at* our expenditure.

✔ We must cut *down* our expenditure.

37. ✘ You are cut out *at* a sailor.

✔ You are cut out *for* a sailor.

38. ✘ She is done *with*.

✔ She is done *for*.

39. ✘ Having walked a long distance, we are quite done *off*.

✔ Having walked a long distance, we are quite done *up*.

40. ✗ This scheme will fall *about* for want of support.

✔ This scheme will fall *through* for want of support.

41. ✗ I have heard that all the brothers have fallen *about.*

✔ I have heard that all the brothers have fallen *out.*

42. ✗ You can not expect to get *of* with a fine.

✔ You can not expect to get *off* with a fine.

43. ✗ The burglars got *at* with my cash box.

✔ The burglars got *away* with my cash box.

44. ✗ She has got *with* her examination.

✔ She has got *through* her examination.

45. ✗ They were fortunate to get out *off* his clutches.

✔ They were fortunate to get out *of* his clutches.

46. ✗ The accused has given himself *off* to the police.

✔ The accused has given himself *up* to the police.

47. ✗ The doctors have given him *of.*

✔ The doctors have given him *up.*

48. ✗ The fire gave *of* a dense smoke.

✔ The fire gave *off* a dense smoke.

49. ✗ The principal gave *way* the prizes.

✔ The principal gave *away* the prizes.

50. ✗ You should give *off* this foolish attempt.

✔ You should give *over* this foolish attempt.

51. ✘ The enemy forces did not give *up* easily.

✔ The enemy forces did not give *in* easily.

52. ✘ He promised to go *in* the matter.

✔ He promised to go *into* the matter.

53. ✘ The auditor went *into* the balance sheet.

✔ The auditor went *over* the balance sheet.

54. ✘ This poor man has gone *with* much.

✔ This poor man has gone *through* much.

55. ✘ They were held *out* by robbers.

✔ They were held *up* by robbers.

56. ✘ She holds *up* no promise of future prospects.

✔ She holds *out* no promise of future prospects.

57. ✘ You should try your best to keep *with* the reputation of your family.

✔ You should try your best to keep *up* the reputation of your family.

58. ✘ We shall keep *off* nothing from you.

✔ We shall keep *back* nothing from you.

59. ✘ They kept *about* talking.

✔ They kept *on* talking.

60. ✘ The furniture was knocked *out* for two thousand rupees.

✔ The furniture was knocked *down* for two thousand rupees.

61. ✘ The enemy soldiers laid *out* their arms.

✔ The enemy soldiers laid *down* their arms.

62. ✘ We must lay *off* our money carefully.

✔ We must lay *out* our money carefully.

63. ✘ She was let *in* my secret.

✔ She was let *into* my secret.

64. ✘ The accused was let *of* with a small fine.

✔ The accused was let *off* with a small fine.

65. ✘ We should not look down *on* the poor.

✔ We should not look down *upon* the poor.

66. ✘ Her uncle looks *at* her.

✔ Her uncle looks *after* her.

67. ✘ You should look *at* the word in the dictionary.

✔ You should look *up* the word in the dictionary.

68. ✘ I will look *to* the matter.

✔ I will look *into* the matter.

69. ✘ I am looking forward *about* the arrival of my son.

✔ I am looking forward *to* the arrival of my son.

70. ✘ She looks *at* me as her son.

✔ She looks *on* me as her son.

71. ✘ Prices of essential commodities are looking *into*.

✔ Prices of essential commodities are looking *up*.

72. ✘ Things are looking *in*.

✔ Things are looking *up*.

73. ✘ Contentment makes *with* happiness.

✔ Contentment makes *for* happiness.

74. ✘ You can not make *about* the meaning of this sentence.

✔ You can not make *out* the meaning of this sentence.

75. ✘ The two brothers who had quarrelled have made it *on*.

✔ The two brothers who had quarrelled have made it *up*.

76. ✘ The sailors passed *with* terrible sufferings.

✔ The sailors passed *through* terrible sufferings.

77. ✘ She passed herself *of* as a noble woman.

✔ She passed herself *off* as a noble woman.

78. ✘ The selection committee picked *up* the best players for the team.

✔ The selection committee picked *out* the best players for the team.

79. ✘ I lost considerable weight in sickness but am now picking *with.*

✔ I lost considerable weight in sickness but am now picking *up.*

80. ✘ You will be pulled *at* by the principal.

✔ You will be pulled *up* by the principal.

81. ✘ Many unauthorized buildings were pulled *off* in Delhi.

✔ Many unauthorized buildings were pulled *down* in Delhi.

82. ✘ The patient has pulled *out.*

✔ The patient has pulled *through.*

83. ✘ My brother pulled *with* the examination.

✔ My brother pulled *through* the examination.

84. ✘ We should not put *up* an air of superiority.

84. ✔ We should not put on an air of superiority

85. ✘ Kindly put off the light.

✔ Kindly put out the light.

86. ✘ Don't try to put me of with promises.

✔ Don't try to put me off with promises.

87. ✘ I have to put of my departure for two days.

✔ I have to put off my departure for two days.

88. ✗ I had to put up in a lot of inconvenience during my journey.

    ✔ I had to put up with a lot of inconvenience during my journey.

89. ✗ I am run out owing to hardwork.

    ✔ I am run down owing to hardwork.

90. ✗ The lease of this house has run down.

    ✔ The lease of this house has run out.

91. ✗ We should not run in debt.

    ✔ We should not run into debt.

92. ✗ I can easily see at your trick.

    ✔ I can easily see through your trick.

93. ✗ I went to sea of my parents.

    ✔ I went to see off my parents.

94. ✗ The Supreme Court set side the decree of the High Court.

    ✔ The Supreme Court set aside the decree of the High Court.

95. ✗ They set of for Mumbai early this morning.

    ✔ They set off for Mumbai early this morning.

96. ✗ This compartment is set part for ladies.

    ✔ This compartment is set apart for ladies.

97. ✗ You should set off your views clearly.

    ✔ You should set forth your views clearly.

98. ✗ Winter in India sets at about November.

    ✔ Winter in India sets in about November.

99. ✗ There is no amenity in this office to speak about.

    ✔ There is no amenity in this office to speak of.

100. ✗ You must stand with me in my difficulty.

✔ You must stand by me in my difficulty.

101. ✘ She is struck down in paralysis.

✔ She is struck down with paralysis.

102. ✘ His name was struck of from the register of medical practitioners.

✔ His name was struck off from the register of medical practitioners.

103. ✘ This furniture takes on too much room.

✔ This furniture takes up too much room.

104. ✘ You take in your mother.

✔ You take after your mother.

105. ✘ It is difficult to take with the meaning of T.S. Eliot's poetry.

✔ It is difficult to take in the meaning of T.S. Eliot's poetry.

106. ✘ Lately he has taken on the consumption of a lot of alcohol.

✔ Lately he has taken to the consumption of a lot of alcohol.

107. ✘ They talked on the matter for two hours.

✔ They talked over the matter for two hours.

108. ✘ Overwork will tell on your health.

✔ Overwork will tell upon your health.

109. ✘ His antecedents told about him.

✔ His antecedents told against him.

110. ✘ The bill was thrown off by the Parliament.

✔ The bill was thrown out by the Parliament.

111. ✘ People throw off all old friends when they become rich.

✔ People throw over all old friends when they become rich.

112. ✘ This factory turns about 10,000 lbs of cloth a day.

✔ This factory turns out 10,000 lbs of cloth a day.

113. ✘ She will turn in to be a good person.

✔ She will turn out to be a good person.

114. ✘ In one's adversity one's very friends turn off one.

✔ In one's adversity one's very friends turn against one.

115. ✘ I can't say what will turn about next.

✔ I can't say what will turn up next.

116. ✘ She had promised to come but she did not turn in.

✔ She had promised to come but she did not turn up.

117. ✘ He can work in a difficult problem in a few minutes.

✔ He can work out a difficult problem in a few minutes.

118. ✘ Nothing worked up in persuading him to accept our advice.

✔ Nothing worked on in persuading him to accept our advice.

119. ✘ Despite her brag she had to eat a humble pie.

✔ Despite her brag she had to eat humble pie.

120. ✘ Don't brag too much, you have *to eat your word.*

✔ Don't brag too much, you have *to eat your words.*

121. ✘ He is *not worthy of his salt.*

✔ He is *not worth his salt.*

122. ✗ The prices have increased so much that she finds it difficult *to make two ends meet.*

✔ The prices have increased so much that she finds it difficult *to make both ends meet.*

123. ✗ The belief in old values is *losing grounds.*

✔ The belief in old values is *losing ground.*

124. ✗ Many Indian soldiers *won their laurel* in Kargil War.

✔ Many Indian soldiers *won their laurels* in Kargil War.

125. ✗ She was received *with open arm.*

✔ She was received *with open arms.*

126. ✗ I can't trust a man who *plays fast and lose.*

✔ I can't trust a man who *plays fast and loose.*

127. ✗ The principal *took the naughty student to tasks.*

✔ The principal *took the naughty student to task.*

128. ✗ The student *turned deaf ears* to the teacher's advice.

✔ The student *turned a deaf ear* to the teacher's advice.

129. ✗ Your argument can not *hold waters.*

✔ Your argument can not *hold water.*

130. ✗ She wants to achieve her object *by hook or crook.*

✔ She wants to achieve her object *by hook or by crook.*

131. ✗ She accepted my statement *without reserves.*

✔ She accepted my statement *without reserve.*

132. ✗ The chairman will *take exception at* your remark.

✔ The chairman will *take exception to* your remark.

133. ✗ This belief is *gaining grounds.*

✔ This belief is *gaining ground.*

134. ✗ I don't believe in *paying of old scores.*

✓ I don't believe in *paying off old scores.*

135. ✗ She has been working *on and of* to complete a story.

✓ She has been working *on and off* to complete a story.

136. ✗ I visit him *of and on.*

✓ I visit him *off and on.*

137. ✗ We should not *put spokes in one's wheels.*

✓ We should not *put a spoke in one's wheel.*

138. ✗ He wants to *make his marks* as a writer.

✓ He wants to *make his mark* as a writer.

139. ✗ Our proposal *fell flats.*

✓ Our proposal *fell flat.*

140. ✗ You should *put your feet down* to improve discipline in this office.

✓ You should *put your foot down* to improve discipline in this office.

141. ✗ I have *made up my minds* to do social service.

✓ I have *made up my mind* to do social service.

142. ✗ There is *no love loose between* the two brothers.

✓ There is *no love lost between* the two brothers.

143. ✗ Many people in the world live *at hand to mouth.*

✔ Many people in the world live *from hand to mouth.*

144. ✗ You are sure to succeed *in long run.*

✔ You are sure to succeed *in the long run.*

145. ✗ No one can *call* his honesty *into question.*

✔ No one can *call* his honesty *in question.*

146. ✗ You came to his rescue *in nick of time.*

✔ You came to his rescue *in the nick of time.*

147. ✗ I will stand by you *through thicks and thins.*

✔ I will stand by you *through thick and thin.*

148. ✗ My friend *threw cold waters on my plans.*

✔ My friend *threw cold water on my plans.*

149. ✗ Many politicians are *hands and gloves* with criminals.

✔ Many politicians are *hand and glove* with criminals.

150. ✗ The investigation has *brought to lights* some startling facts.

✔ The investigation has *brought to light* some startling facts.

151. ✗ You will *burn your finger* if you interfere in others' affairs.

✔ You will *burn your fingers* if you interfere in others' affairs.

152. ✗ The minister *strained all nerves* to get his son elected.

✔ The minister strained *every nerve* to get his son elected.

153. ✗ On hearing the news of his father's arrival, he was *besides himself* with joy.

✔ On hearing the news of his father's arrival, he was *beside himself* with joy.

154. ✗ Every thing seems to be *at six and seven* in this house.

✔ Every thing seems to be *at sixes and sevens* in this house.

155. ✘ Don't *give yourself air.*

✔ Don't *give yourself airs.*

156. ✘ Retrenchment is the *order of the days* in every public and private office.

✔ Retrenchment is the *order of the day* in every public and private office.

157. ✘ One must *keep paces with* the changing times.

✔ One must *keep pace with* the changing times.

158. ✘ This book of physics is quite *out of dates.*

✔ This book of physics is quite *out of date.*

159. ✘ This is the most *up to dates* book on the subject.

✔ This is the most *up to date* book on the subject.

MAD ABOUT PHYSICS
Braintwisters, Paradoxes, and Curiosities
Christopher P. Jargodzki and Franklin Potter

160. ✘ The book written by you *speaks volumes for* the hardwork done by you.

✔ The book written by you *speaks volume for* the hardwork done by you.

161. ✘ The doctors are *hoping against hopes* about the recovery of the patient.

✔ The doctors are *hoping against hope* about the recovery of the patient.

162. ✘ Your ignoble deeds will get you *in hot waters.*

✔ Your ignoble deeds will get you *into hot water.*

163. ✘ Our forces *got the best of* the Pakistani forces in Kargil War.

✔ Our forces *got the better* of the Pakistani forces in Kargil War.

164. ✘ The accused *got of easy.*

✔ The accused *got off easy.*

165. ✗ He *washed his hand off* the whole matter.

✔ He *washed his hands of* the whole matter.

166. ✗ The situation has *gone out of hands.*

✔ The situation has *gone out of hand.*

167. ✗ I will try my best to *hit the nails on the head.*

✔ I will try my best to *hit the nail on the head.*

168. ✗ He seems to be *in high spirit* today.

✔ He seems to be *in high spirits* today.

169. ✗ Why are you *out of spirit*?

✔ Why are you *out of spirits*?

170. ✗ He seems to have *his axe to grind.*

✔ He seems to have *an axe to grind.*

171. ✗ The news of the Prime Minister's death *spread like a wild fire.*

✔ The news of the Prime Minister's death *spread like wild fire.*

172. ✗ She *took to her heart* the death of her husband.

✔ She *took to heart* the death of her husband.

173. ✗ The life was *thrown out of gears* due to the strike.

✔ The life was *thrown out of gear* due to the strike.

174. ✘ He is not an orator but he has *a gift of the gab.*

✔ He is not an orator but he has *the gift of the gab.*

175. ✘ His proposal *did not go home for the* directors.

✔ His proposal *did not go home to the* directors.

176. ✘ These days many people are interested in *coining rupees.*

✔ These days many people are interested in *coining money.*

177. ✘ He is *in good book of* the principal.

✔ He is *in the good books* of the principal.

178. ✘ You should *put your feet down* in your decision.

✔ You should *put your foot down* in your decision.

179. ✘ He invited me to dinner but I had to *foot the bills.*

✔ He invited me to dinner but I had to *foot the bill.*

180. ✘ You must fight *teeth and nails* for your rights.

✔ You must fight *tooth and nail* for your rights.

181. ✘ This property belonged to me but it has *changed hand* recently.

✔ This property belonged to me but it has *changed hands* recently.

182. ✘ The robbers *took to their heel* on seeing the policemen.

✔ The robbers *took to their heels* on seeing the policemen.

183. ✘ My house is *in a stone's throw of* the church.

✔ My house is *within a stone's throw of* the church.

184. ✘ *Keep on touch with* the latest developments.

✔ *Keep in touch with* the latest developments.

185. ✗ Don't keep me *in dark* about the affairs of this office.

✓ Don't keep me *in the dark* about the affairs of this office.

186. ✗ She has *so many irons in the fire.*

✓ She has *too many irons in the fire.*

187. ✗ The soldiers were *true in their salt.*

✓ The soldiers were *true to their salt.*

188. ✗ You seem to be *in your wits end.*

✓ You seem to be *at your wits end.*

189. ✗ You should *give ears to* the teacher.

✓ You should *give ear to* the teacher.

190. ✗ This fashion is *in air.*

✓ This fashion is in *the air.*

191. ✗ This poem is meant *to be read between line.*

✓ This poem is meant *to be read between the lines.*

192. ✗ Many persons were killed *in the cold blood.*

✓ Many persons were killed *in cold blood.*

193. ✗ I want your terms *in the black and white.*

✓ I want your terms *in black and white.*

194. ✗ I *smell rats.*

✓ I *smell a rat.*

195. ✗ We should *nip the evil in bud.*

✓ We should *nip the evil in the bud.*

196. ✗ To implement your proposal is *out of question.*

✓ To implement your proposal is *out of the question.*

197. ✗ Your performance was *up to mark.*

✓ Your performance was *up to the mark*

198. ✗ *The long and short of it* is that I am not interested in teaching you.

✔ *The long and the short of it* is that I am not interested in teaching you.

199. ✘ He *changed colours* when the police inspector questioned him about his antecedents.

✔ He *changed colour* when the police inspector questioned him about his antecedents.

200. ✘ You should *take stocks of* the whole situation.

✔ You should *take stock of* the whole situation.

201. ✘ The election campaign for the Delhi University is *in the full swing.*

✔ The election campaign for the Delhi University is *in full swing.*

202. ✘ Pt. Jawahar Lal Nehru was *born with silver spoons in his mouth.*

✔ Pt. Jawahar Lal Nehru was *born with a silver spoon in his mouth.*

203. ✘ This computer *has stood me in a good stead.*

✔ This computer *has stood me in good stead.*

204. ✘ The teacher *took the naughty boy to tasks.*

✔ The teacher *took the naughty boy to task.*

205. ✘ He can't meet you now, as *his hand is full.*

✔ He can't meet you now, as *his hands are full.*

206. ✘ All our efforts *ended in a smoke.*

✔ All our efforts *ended in smoke.*

207. ✘ The police *left no stones unturned* to nab the terrorists.

✔ The police *left no stone unturned* to nab the terrorists.

208. ✘ He has decided *to rest on his laurel.*

✔ He has decided *to rest on his laurels.*

209. ✘ I am fed up with his *harping on the same strings.*

✔ I am fed up with his *harping on the same string.*

210. ✗ Your performance was *as good as the gold.*

✔ Your performance was *as good as gold.*

211. ✗ He has *to make good the losses.*

✔ He has *to make good the loss.*

212. ✗ Don't *kick up the row.*

✔ Don't *kick up a row.*

213. ✗ She was *as good as her* words.

✔ She was *as good as her word.*

214. ✗ She seems *ill at a ease.*

✔ She seems *ill at ease.*

215. ✗ This man is *heard of hearing.*

✔ This man is *hard of hearing.*

216. ✗ Daniel is *on his last leg.*

✔ Daniel is *on his last legs.*

217. ✗ I can make *nether heads nor tails* of your answer.

✔ I can make *neither head nor tail* of your answer.

218. ✗ By speaking against the democracy, he has *stirred hornets' nest.*

✔ By speaking against the democracy, he has *stirred up a hornets' nest*

219. ✗ He is *all inches* a noble man.

✔ He is *every inch* a nobleman.

220. ✗ You must prove your worth by *rising to the occasions.*

✔ You must prove your worth by *rising to the occasion.*

221. ✗ Provide me *the in and out* of this affair.

✔ Provide me *the ins and outs* of this affair.

222. ✗ She is *over heads and ears* in debt.

✔ She is *over head and ears* in debt.

223. ✘ *Beyond all questions,* he is a gentleman.

✔ *Beyond all question,* he is a gentleman.

224. ✘ Intimate friends need not *stand in ceremony.*

✔ Intimate friends need not *stand on ceremony.*

225. ✘ I went *out of my ways* to help him.

✔ I *went out of my way* to help him.

226. ✘ The proposal was accepted *with single voice.*

✔ The proposal was accepted *with one voice.*

227. ✘ The fate of the accused *hangs in balance.*

✔ The fate of the accused *hangs in the balance.*

228. ✘ She *was carried of her feet* when she knew her result.

✔ She *was carried off her feet* when she knew her result.

229. ✘ You should *make most of your* opportunity.

✔ You should *make the most of your opportunity.*

230. ✘ I felt *like a fish out of the water* when they started discussing politics.

✔ I felt *like a fish out of water* when they started discussing politics.

231. ✘ You should not study *by fits and by starts.*

✔ You should not study *by fits and starts.*

232. ✘ He has become rich and now *takes things easily.*

✔ He has become rich and now *takes things easy.*

233. ✘ They *took into accounts* his vast experience and gave him appointment letter.

✔ They *took into account* his vast experience and gave him appointment letter.

234. ✘ You cannot expect a definite reply *at the spur of the moment.*

✔ You cannot expect a definite reply *on the spur of the moment.*

235. ✘ She took her failure *to her heart.*

✔ She took her failure *to heart.*

236. ✘ He will leave India *for the good.*

✔ He will leave India *for good.*

237. ✘ You can expect me to be *at your back* and *call.*

✔ You can expect me to be *at your beck* and *call.*

238. ✘ You should not *burn the candle from both ends.*

✔ You should not *burn the candle at both ends.*

239. ✘ We should *bury the hatchets* and work for the betterment of the office.

✔ We should *bury the hatchet* and work for the betterment of the office.

240. ✘ He seems to be *feathering his own nests.*

✔ He seems to be *feathering his own nest.*

241. ✘ Some hooligans *lay hands on him* when he was going to office.

✔ Some hooligans *laid hands on him* when he was going to office.

242. ✘ It is suspected that he *has hands in the plot.*

✔ It is suspected that *he has a hand* in the plot.

243. ✘ He is in the habit of *blowing his own trumpets.*

✔ He is in the habit of *blowing his own trumpet.*

244. ✘ I am *heads and shoulders* in debt.

✔ I am *head and shoulders* in debt.

245. ✘ The foolish prince *made ducks and drake* of his patrimony.

✔ The foolish prince *made ducks and drakes* of his patrimony.

246. ✗ You *should try your hands* in business.

✔ You *should try your hand* in business.

247. ✗ During his adversity even his best friends *gave him the cold shoulders.*

✔ During his adversity even his best friends *gave him the cold shoulder.*

248. ✗ The chairman urged the members to take drastic action but they *hanged fire.*

✔ The chairman urged the members to take drastic action but they *hung fire.*

249. ✗ We were *all the ears* during his speech.

✔ We were *all ears* during his speech.

250. ✗ I was *all eye* to see what they would do.

✔ I was *all eyes* to see what they would do.

251. ✗ Having a large family makes it difficult for him *to keep his hands above water.*

✔ Having a large family makes it difficult for him *to keep his hand above water.*

252. ✗ You will never *set the Thames on the fire.*

✔ You will never *set the Thames on fire.*

253. ✗ You will *come to griefs* if you don't work hard.

✔ You will *come to grief* if you don't work hard.

254. ✗ You should keep the fellow *at arm length.*

✔ You should keep the fellow *at arm's length.*

255. ✗ He is leaving his hometown *bags and baggage.*

✔ He is leaving his hometown *bag and baggage.*

256. ✘ The account of the murder *made her blood creeps.*

✔ The account of the murder *made her blood creep.*

257. ✘ Kashmir is *a bone of contentions* between India and Pakistan.

✔ Kashmir is *a bone of contention* between India and Pakistan.

258. ✘ After his victory in elections, he has become *swollen head.*

✔ After his victory in elections, he has become *swollen-headed.*

259. ✘ She *took up the cudgel for* her companion.

✔ She *took up the cudgels for* her companion.

260. ✘ This law is *dead letter.*

✔ This law is *a dead letter.*

261. ✘ The two brothers don't *see eyes to eyes* on many new proposals.

✔ The two brothers don't *see eye to eye* on many new proposals.

262. ✘ The story of the shipwreck made *his flesh creeps.*

✔ The story of the shipwreck made *his flesh creep.*

263. ✘ He *pins his faith on* technical education.

✔ He *pins his faith to* technical education.

264. ✘ You are *a great hand in* organizing public meetings.

✔ You are *a great hand at* organizing public meetings.

265. ✘ Many people have embraced Islam for *loaves and fish.*

✔ Many people have embraced Islam for *loaves and fishes.*

266. ✘ His wife *left him in lurch.*

✔ His wife *left him in the lurch.*

267. ✘ Your observations are *besides the mark.*

✔ Your observations are *beside the mark.*

268. ✘ His enemies *moved heavens and earths* to unseat him.

✔ His enemies *moved heaven and earth* to unseat him.

269. ✘ You should *stick to your colour.*

✔ You should *stick to your colours.*

270. ✘ Employment problem is hard nut to crack.

✔ Employment problem is a hard nut to crack.

271. ✘ The agitators are *playing with the fire.*

✔ The agitators are *playing with fire.*

272. ✘ He generally does not *put his hands in his pockets.*

✔ He generally does not *put his hand in his pocket.*

273. ✘ These days wearing scanty clothes is *all rage.*

✔ These days wearing scanty clothes is *all the rage.*

274. ✘ Your letter to your ward *speaks volumes of* your forbearance.

✔ Your letter to your ward *speaks volumes for* your forbearance..

275. ✘ You don't look *quite up to* mark today.

✔ You don't look *quite up to the mark* today.

276. ✘ The judge was a learned man who could *put twos and twos together.*

✔ The judge was a learned man who could *put two and two together.*

277. ✘ You have *two strings to your bows.*

✔ You have *two strings to your bow.*

278. ✘ Her uncle has taken her *under his wings.*

✔ Her uncle has taken her *under his wing.*

279. ✘ I think we have been sent on *a wild-geese chase.*

✔ I think we have been sent on *a wild-goose chase.*

280. ✘ You are likely to be in hot waters because of your present deeds.

✔ You are likely to be *in hot water* because of your present deeds.

281. ✘ Do not *wash your dirty linen in the public.*

✔ Do not *wash your dirty linen in public.*

282. ✘ The two brothers are *at dagger drawn.*

✔ The two brothers are *at daggers drawn.*

283. ✘ Mahatma Gandhi has done *yeoman service* in the freedom struggle of India.

✔ Mahatma Gandhi has done *yeoman's service* in the freedom struggle of India.

284. ✘ He is *at the wrong side of sixty.*

✔ He is *on the wrong side of sixty.*

285. ✘ He is a *man of his words.*

✔ He is a *man of his word.*

286. ✘ He is a *wolf in sheep clothing.*

✔ He is a *wolf in sheep's clothing.*

287. ✘ Don't keep him *on tenderhook.*

✔ Don't keep him *on tenderhooks.*

288. ✘ Some of the students *shook in their shoe* when the Inspector entered the class.

✔ Some of the students *shook in their shoes* when the Inspector entered the class.

289. ✘ There are *black sheeps in all communities.*

✔ There are *black sheep* in all communities.

290. ✘ Although the leader of the Opposition was unmercifully heckled, he *stood to his gun*.

✔ Although the leader of the Opposition was unmercifully heckled, he *stood to his guns*.

CLUES

1. Blow over (pass off)
2. Backed up– (supported)
2. Bear out- (substantiate)
4. Cleared up- (explained)
5. Dispose of- (sell)
6. Eaten away- (corroded)
7. Fixed upon- (chose)
8. Gained on- (won the favour of)
9. Growing upon- (is having stronger and stronger hold)
10. Hear out- (hear to the end)
11. Hit upon– (found)
12. Hanging about– (loitering about)
13. Led up to- (culminated in)
14. Prevail on–(persuade)
15. Shake off- (get rid of)
16. Stick out for – (persists in demanding)
17. Trumped up - (concocted, fabricated)
18. Bore away- (Won)
19. Bear up- (support)
20. Bear with- (have patience with)
21. Broke into- (entered by force)
22. Brought out- (published)
23. Bring round (convert)
24. Call for– (demand)

25. Call in (summon)
26. Call on– (pay a brief visit)
27. Call up (recollect)
28. Carried out– (executed)
29. Carry on– (manage)
30. Carried off – (killed)
31. Come about– (happen)
32. Come by– (get)
33. Come up- (will be raised for discussion)
34. Cried out against- (protested against)
35. Cut off- (died)
36. Cut down- (reduce)
37. Cut out for– (specially fitted to be)
38. Done for– (ruined)
39. Done up-(exhausted, fatigued)
40. Fall through– (fail)
41. Fallen out- (quarrelled)
42. Get off– (escape)
43. Got away - (escaped)
44. Got through– (passed)
45. Get out of- (escape from)
46. Give oneself up- (have no hope of recovery).
48. Gave off– (emitted)
49. Gave away- (distributed)
50. Give over- (abandon)
51. Give in- (submit, yield)
52. Go into- (examine)
53. Went over–(examined)
54. Gone through- (suffered)

55. Held up- (stopped on the way and robbed)
56. Hold out– (give)
57. Keep up- (carry on)
58. Keep back– (conceal)
59. Kept on– (continued)
60. Knocked down– (sold at an auction)
61. Laid down– (surrendered)
62. Lay out– (invest)
63. Let into – (made acquainted with)
64. Let off- (punished leniently)
65. Look down upon– (despise)
66. Look after– (take care of)
67. Look up– (search for)
68. Look into– (investigate)
69. Look forward to – (expect with pleasure)
70. Look on– (regard)
71. Look up– (rise)
72. Look up– (improve)
73. Make for– (conduce to)
74. Make out– (discover)
75. Made it up– (become reconciled)
76. Passed through– (underwent)
77. Passed herself off– (pretended to be)
78. Picked out– (selected)
79. Picking up – (improving)
80. Pulled up– (scolded, rebuked)
81. Pulled down– (demolished)
82. Pulled through– (recovered from illness)
83. Pulled through (Passed with difficulty)

84. Put on– (assume)
85. Put out- (extinguish)
86. Put off-(evade)
87. Put off- (postpone)
88. Put up with- (tolerate)
89. Run down- (enfeebled)
90. Run out- (expired, came to an end)
91. Run into- (incur)
92. See through- (detect)
93. See off- (witness the departure)
94. Set aside- (annulled)
95. Set off- (started)
96. Set apart- (reserved)
97. Set forth- (explain)
98. Sets in- (begins)
99. Speak of- (worth mentioning)
100. Stand by- (support)
101. Struck down with- (attacked by)
102. Struck off- (removed)
103. Takes up- (occupies)
104. Take after- (resemble)
105. Take in- (understand, comprehend)
106. Taken to- (become addicted to)
107. Talked over- (discussed)
108. Tell upon- (affect).
109. Told against- (proved unfavourable to).
110. Thrown out- (rejected).
111. Throw over- (abandon).

112. Turns out- (produces).
113. Turn out- (prove).
114. Turn against- (become hostile).
115. Turn up- (happen).
116. Turn up- (appear).
117. Work out- (solve).
118. Worked on- (influenced).
119. To eat humble pie- (to apologize humbly).
120. To eat your words- (to retract your statement, to take back what you have said).
121. Not worth his salt- (quite worthless).
122. To make both ends meet- (to live within income).
123. Losing ground- (becoming less powerful or acceptable.
124. Won their laurels- (acquired destination or glory).
125. With open arms- (with a warm welcome).
126. Plays fast and loose- (says one thing and does another).
127. Took to task- (rebuked).
128. Turned a deaf ear- (disregarded).
129. Hold water- (stand scrutiny, is unsound,).
130. By hook or by crook- (by fair means or foul)
131. Without reserve- (fully implicitly).
132. Take exception to- (object to)
133. Gaining ground-(becoming more general).
134. Paying off old scores (having revenge).
135. On and off- (at intervals).
136. Put a spoke in one's wheels- (thwart in the execution of design).
137. Make his mark- (distinguish himself).

138. at his fingers' ends- (knew it thoroughly).
139. Fell flat- (met with cold reception).
140. Put your foot down- (take a resolute stand).
141. Made up my mind- (resolved, decided).
142. No love lost- (not on good terms).
143. From hand to mouth- (without any provision for the future.
144. In the long run – (eventually, ultimately).
145. (Call in question – (challenge, express a doubt about).
146. In the nick of time- (Just at the right moment).
147. Through thick and thin- (under all conditions).
148. Threw cold water on my plans- (discouraged me by showing indifference).
149. Hand and glove- (on very intimate terms).
150. Brought to light- (disclosed).
151. Burn your fingers- (get yourself into trouble).
152. Strained every nerve- (used his utmost efforts).
153. Beside himself with joy- (out of his mind).
154. At sixes and sevens- (in disorder or confusion).
155. Give yourself airs- (behave arrogantly).
156. Order of the day- (the prevailing state of things).
157. Keep pace with- (progress at equal rate with).
158. Out of date- (obsolete).
159. Up-to-date- (modern, recent).
160. Speaks volumes for- (serves as a strong testimony to).
161. Hoping against hope- (hoping even when the case seems hopeless).
162. Into hot water- (into trouble).
163. Got the better of- (overcame).

164. Got off easy- (got a light sentence).
165. Washed his hands of- (refused to have anything more to do with it).
166. Gone out of hand- (beyond control).
167. Hit the nail on the head- (say or do exactly the right thing).
168. In high spirits- (cheerful, joyful).
169. Out of spirits- (gloomy, sad).
170. An axe to grind- (private ends to serve, a personal interest in the matter).
171. Spread like wild fire- (spread rapidly).
172. Took to heart- (was deeply affected by).
173. The gift of the gab- (a talent for speaking).
174. Thrown out of gear- (disturbed the working of) .
175. Did not go home- (did not appeal).
176. Coining money- (making money rapidly, earning large sums easily).
177. In the good books of- (in favour with).
178. Put your foot down- (remain firm, refuse to yield).
179. Foot the bill- (pay for it).
180. Tooth and nail- (with all your power).
181. Changed hands- (became someone else's property).
182. Took to their heels- (ran off).
183. Within a stone's throw-(a short distance)
184. Keep in touch with- (have intimate knowledge of).
185. In the dark- (in ignorance).
186. Too many irons in the fire- (engaged in too many enterprises at the same time).
187. True to their salt- (faithful to their employers).

188. At your wit's end- (quite puzzled, at a complete loss how to act.).

189. Give ear to- (listen to).

190. In the air- (prevalent, found everywhere).

191. To be read between the lines- (it has a hidden or unexpressed meaning not apparent on the surface).

192. In cold blood- (not in the heat of passion or excitement but deliberately).

193. In black and white- (in writing).

194. Smell a rat- (have reason to suspect something).

195. Nip the evil in the bud- (make it fail before it can mature).

196. Out of the question- (not to be thought of, impossible).

197. Upto the mark- (quite satisfactory).

198. The long and the short of it- (the simple fact, the whole matter in a few words).

199. Changed colour- (turned pale).

200. Take stock of- (survey).

201. In full swing- (very active).

202. Born with a silver spoon in his mouth- (born in wealth and luxury).

203. In good stead- (proved useful).

204. Took to task- (reproved).

205. His hands are full- (is very busy).

206. Ended in smoke- (came to nothing).

207. Left no stone unturned- (used all available means, adopted every possible method of search).

208. To rest on his laurels- (to retire from active life).

209. Harping on the same string- (dwell tediously on the same subject).

210. As good as her word- (Kept her promise).
211. As good as gold- (very good).
212. To make good the loss- (to compensate for the loss).
213. Kick up a row- (make great noise or fuss).
214. Ill at ease- (uneasy, anxious, uncomfortable).
215. Hard of hearing- (somewhat deaf).
216. On his last legs- (on the verge of ruin).
217. Neither head nor tail- (nothing).
218. Stirred up a hornets' nest- (excited the hostility or adverse criticism of a large number of people).
219. Every inch- (entirely, completely).
220. By rising to the occasion - (show yourself equal to dealing with the emergency).
221. The ins and outs- (the full details).
222. Head and ears- (deeply).
223. Beyond all question- (undoubtedly).
224. Stand on ceremony- (act with reserve, insist on strict rules of etiquette being observed).
225. Went out of my way- (took special trouble).
226. With one voice- (unanimously).
227. Hangs in the balance- (is undecided).
228. Was carried off her feet- (was wild with excitement).
229. Make the most of- (use it to the best advantage).
230. Like a fish out of water- (like one out of his element, in a strange situation).
231. By fits and starts- (irregularly, without steady application).
232. Takes things easy- (does not work hard).
233. Took into account- (considered).

234. On the spur of the moment- (at once, without deliberation).
235. Took to heart- (felt it deeply).
236. For good- (permanently).
237. At your beck and call- (under your absolute control).
238. Burn the candle at both ends- (overtax your energies).
239. Bury the hatchet- (cease fighting, make peace).
240. Feathering his own nest- (making money unfairly).
241. Laid hands on- (assaulted).
242. Has a hand- (is concerned in).
243. Blowing his own trumpet- (praising himself).
244. Head and shoulders- (very much).
245. Made ducks and drakes- (squandered).
246. Should try your hand- (make an attempt).
247. Gave him the cold shoulder- (treated him in a cold and distant manner).
248. Hung fire- (were reluctant, hesitated).
249. All ears- (deeply attentive).
250. All eyes- (eagerly watching).
251. To keep his hand above water- (to keep out of debt).
252. Set the Thames on fire- (do some remarkable or surprising thing).
253. Come to grief- (will be ruined).
254. At arm's length- (at a distance, hold aloof from).
255. Bag and baggage- (with all belongings, altogether, completely).
256. Made her blood creep- (filled her with horror).
257. A bone of contention- (a subject of dispute).
258. Swollen - headed - (conceited).

259. Took up the cudgels- (defended vigorously).

260. A dead letter- (no longer in force).

261. See eye to eye- (to be in complete agreement).

262. Made his flesh creep- (horrified him).

263. Pins his faith to- (places full reliance upon).

264. A great hand at- (expert at)

265. Loaves and fishes- (material benefits).

266. Left him in the lurch- (deserted him in his difficulties).

267. Beside the mark- (not to the point, irrelevant).

268. Moved heaven and earth- (made every possible effort).

269. Stick to your colours- (refuse to yield, be faithful to the cause).

270. A hard nut to crack- (a difficult problem to solve).

271. Playing with fire- (trifling ignorantly with matters liable to cause trouble or suffering).

272. Put his hand in his pocket- (give money in charity).

273. All the rage (extremely popular).

274. Speaks volumes for- (serves as strong testimony to).

275. Quite upto the mark- (in excellent health).

276. Put two and two together- (draw a correct inference, reason logically).

277. Two strings to your bow- (have two sources of income to rely upon).

278. Under his wing- (under his protection).

279. A wild-goose chase- (a foolish and fruitless search).

280. In hot water- (in trouble).

281. Wash your dirty linen in public- (discuss unpleasant private matters before strangers).

282. At daggers drawn- (their relations are strained).

283. Yeomon's service- (excellent work).
284. On the wrong side of sixty- (more than sixty years of age).
285. A man of his word- (a man to be depended upon, a trustworthy person).
286. A wolf in sheep's clothing- (hypocrite).
287. On tenderhooks- (in a state of suspense and anxiety).
288. Shook in their shoes- (trembled with fear).
289. Black sheep- (bad characters, scoundrels).
290. Stood to his guns- (maintained his own opinion)

14

Errors in the Use of Homonyms

A homonym is a word with almost the same pronunciation as another but with a different meaning. The unwary writers use one for another as these homonyms go in pairs and become the cause of errors and confusion. As they appear Synonyms, homonyms pose a great difficulty and pitfall.

Below is given a list of often confusing pairs of words to help the reader, to avoid the use of wrong word:

1. ✘ He will *except* my invitation.
   ✔ He will *accept* my invitation.
2. ✘ All were present *accept* Daniel.
   ✔ All were present *except* Daniel.
3. ✘ I have no *excess* to the Principal.
   ✔ I have no *access* to the Principal.
4. ✘ *Access* of everything is bad.
   ✔ *Excess* of everything is bad.
5. ✘ She has *adapted* a child.
   ✔ She has *adopted* a child.

6. ✘ We must *adopt* ourselves to the changing times.
   ✔ We must *adapt* ourselves to the changing times.

7. ✗ She is *adapt* in painting.

   ✔ She is *adept* in painting.

8. ✗ He will *advice* me.

   ✔ He will *advise* me.

9. ✗ He will give me *advise*.

   ✔ He will give me *advice*.

10. ✗ Heavy drinking will *effect* your health.

    ✔ Heavy drinking will *affect* your health.

11. ✗ My advice had no *affect* on him.

    ✔ My advice had no *effect* on him.

12. ✗ Many new reforms were *affected* by the new government.

    ✔ Many new reforms were *effected* by the new government.

13. ✗ You are the legal *air* to the ancestral property.

    ✔ You are the legal *heir* to the ancestral property.

14. ✗ I lighted camphor at the *alter* of the God.

    ✔ I lighted camphor at the *altar* of the God.

15. ✗ I don't *altar* my decisions.

    ✔ I don't *alter* my decisions.

16. ✗ I saw an *angle* in my dream.

    ✔ I saw an *angel* in my dream.

17. ✗ I have learnt the formation of 90° *angle*.

    ✔ I have learnt the formation of 90° *angle*.

18. ✗ I can't *bare* this insult.

    ✔ I can't *bear* this insult.

19. ✗ I saw a *beer* in the zoo.

    ✔ I saw a *bear* in the zoo.

20. ✗ The trees have become *bear.*
    ✔ The trees have become *bare.*
21. ✗ You should get a *birth* reserved.
    ✔ You should get a *berth* reserved.
22. ✗ He is handicapped by *berth.*
    ✔ He is handicapped by *birth.*
23. ✗ He was *borne* in a rich family.
    ✔ He was *born* in a rich family.
24. ✗ It should be *born* in mind that honesty is the best policy.
    ✔ It should be *borne* in mind that honesty is the best policy.
25. ✗ He applied the *break* of the car.
    ✔ He applied the *brake* of the car.
26. ✗ He can *brake* this stone.
    ✔ He can *break* this stone.
27. ✗ She has purchased a *bridle* dress.
    ✔ She has purchased a *bridal* dress.
28. ✗ Control the *bridal* of the horse carefully.
    ✔ Control the *bridle* of the horse carefully.
29. ✗ You should *canvas* for my party.
    ✔ You should *canvass* for my party.
30. ✗ Various governments have failed to *cheque* corruption in the country.
    ✔ Various governments have failed to *check* corruption in the country.
31. ✗ You will receive the payment through *check.*
    ✔ You will receive the payment through *cheque.*
32. ✗ The peon is *ceiling* the letters.
    ✔ The peon is *sealing* the letters.

33. ✘ The *sealing* of this house is very weak.

✔ The *ceiling* of the house is very weak.

34. ✘ Love is a *compliment* to life.

✔ Love is a *complement* to life.

35. ✘ Pay my *complements* to him.

✔ Pay my *compliments* to him.

36. ✘ The mater will be discussed in the Legislative *Counsel.*

✔ The matter will be discussed in the Legislative *Council.*

37. ✘ You should not ignore the *council* of your parents.

✔ You should not ignore the *counsel* of your parents.

38. ✘ You should follow the right *coarse.*

✔ You should follow the right *course.*

39. ✘ This institute teaches a computer *coarse.*

✔ This institute teaches a computer *course.*

40. ✘ This shirt is made of a *course* cloth.

✔ This shirt is made of a *coarse* cloth.

41. ✘ All human beings are *deer* to God.

✔ All human beings are *dear* to God.

42. ✘ We saw a herd of *dear* in the zoo.

✔ We saw a herd of *deer* in the zoo.

43. ✘ You should take only one *doze* of this medicine everyday.

✔ You should take only one *dose* of this medicine everyday.

44. ✘ You should not *dose* while you are studying.

✔ You should not *doze* while you are studying.

45. ✘ I went to the World Book *Fare.*

✔ I went to the World Book *Fair.*

46. ✘ You should pay the taxi *fair*.

✔ You should pay the taxi *fare*.

47. ✘ One should make a *fare* distribution of one's wealth.

✔ One should make a *fair* distribution of one's wealth.

48. ✘ My office is located at the ground *flour*.

✔ My office is located at the ground *floor*.

49. ✘ How much *floor* did you buy?

✔ How much *flour* did you buy?

50. ✘ At the sight of the tiger, the boy ran with *freight*.

✔ At the sight of the tiger the boy ran with *fright*.

51. ✘ You have to pay the *fright* at the counter.

✔ You have to pay the *freight* at the counter.

52. ✘ Some people do not like wearing *guilt* ornaments.

✔ Some people do not like wearing *gilt* ornaments.

53. ✘ He confessed his *gilt* before the magistrate.

✔ He confessed his *guilt* before the magistrate.

54. ✘ His chief *gaol* in life is to become a pilot.

✔ His chief *goal* in life is to become a pilot.

55. ✘ The accused was sent to the goal.

✔ The accused was sent to the gaol.

56. ✘ She has *thick* black *heir*.

✔ She has thick black *hair*.

57. ✘ She is an *hare* to her father's property.

✔ She is an *heir* to her father's property.

58. ✘ The *hair* was running very fast.

✔ The *hare* was running very fast.

59. ✘ I am *hail* and hearty.

✔ I am *hale* and hearty.

60. ✗ I *hale* from Himachal Pradesh.

✔ I *hail* from Himachal Pradesh.

61. ✗ I have pain in my *heal.*

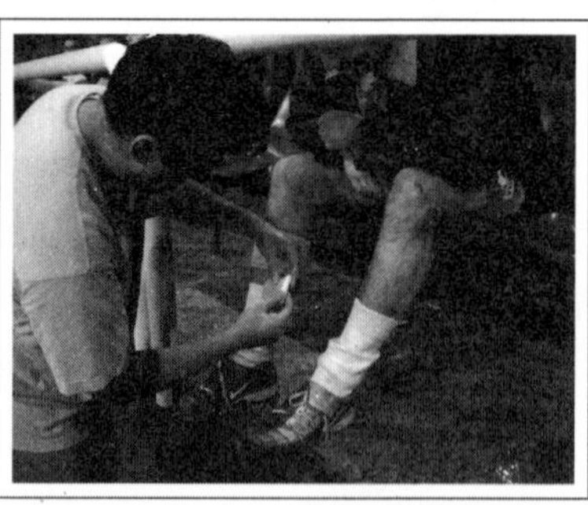

✔ I have pain in my *heel.*

62. ✗ Your wounds will *heel* soon.

✔ Your wounds will *heal* soon.

63. ✗ There is a *whole* in this corner.

✔ There is a *hole* in this corner.

64. ✗ He narrated the *hole* story before the magistrate.

✔ He narrated the *whole* story before the magistrate.

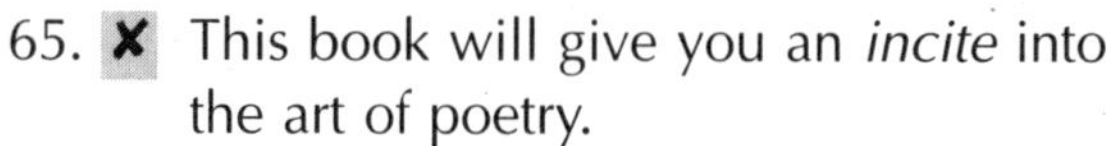

65. ✗ This book will give you an *incite* into the art of poetry.

✔ This book will give you an *insight* into the art of poetry.

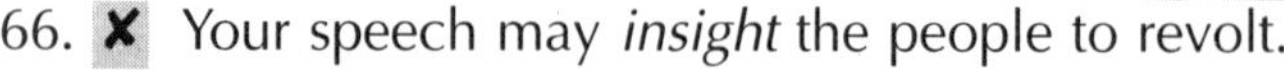

66. ✗ Your speech may *insight* the people to revolt.

✔ Your speech may *incite* the people to revolt.

67. ✗ She arrived *latter* than expected.

✔ She arrived *later* than expected.

68. ✗ The *later* part of this book is boring.

✔ The *latter* part of the book is boring.

69. ✗ He will *loose* money in business.

✔ He will *lose* money in business.

70. ✗ You should not *madal* in others' affairs.

✔ You should not *meddle* in others' affairs.

71. ✗ He received a *meddle* in sports.

✔ He received a *medal* in sports.

72. ✘ The job of a *minor* is a difficult one.

✔ The job of a *miner* is a difficult one.

73. ✘ She is a *knotty* girl.

✔ She is a *naughty* girl.

74. ✘ Every one has to face *naughty* problems in life.

✔ Every one has to face *knotty* problems in life.

75. ✘ It was a *miner* operation.

✔ It was a *minor* operation.

76. ✘ *Nun* of us can solve this sum.

✔ *None* of us can solve this sum.

77. ✘ She has decided to remain *none* till her death.

✔ She has decided to remain *nun* till her death.

78. ✘ The soldiers obeyed the *ardour* of the captain.

✔ The soldiers obeyed the *order* of the captain.

79. ✘ You have developed *order* for English drama.

✔ You have developed *ardour* for English drama.

80. ✘ He purchased a *pare* of shoes.

✔ He purchased a *pair* of shoes.

81. ✘ She *peared* the paper with scissors.

✔ She *pared* the paper with scissors.

82. ✘ I like eating *pairs.*

✔ I like eating *pears.*

83. ✘ You can eat this *peace* of bread.

✔ You can eat this *piece* of bread.

84. ✘ Many people enjoy no *piece* in life.

✔ Many people enjoy no *peace* in life.

85. ✘ We should *prey* to God for health and happiness.

✔ We should *pray* to God for health and happiness.

86. ✘ The wicked person is looking up for a fresh *pray.*

✔ The wicked person is looking up for a fresh *prey.*

87. ✘ The *principle* is likely to arrive soon.

✔ The *principal* is likely to arrive soon.

88. ✘ He is a man of *principals.*

✔ He is a man of *principles.*

89. ✘ Buddha was a great *profit.*

✔ Buddha was a great *prophet.*

90. ✘ He has earned huge *prophet* in business.

✔ He has earned huge *profit* in business.

91. ✘ I am *quiet* happy today.

✔ I am *quite* happy-today.

92. ✘ Pull out the plant with its *rout.*

✔ Pull out the plant with the *root.*

93. ✘ The Congress will *route* BJP in the coming elections.

✔ The Congress will *rout* BJP in the coming elections.

94. ✘ This is my usual bus *root.*

✔ This is my usual bus *route.*

95. ✗ Several people were killed in the *ryots.*

✔ Several people were killed in the *riots.*

96. ✗ This place is calm and *quite.*

✔ This place is calm and *quiet.*

97. ✗ His father is a *riot.*

✔ His father is a *ryot.*

98. ✗ The ship sank into the *see.*

✔ The ship sank into the *sea.*

99. ✗ I don't *sea* anything noble in your action.

✔ I don't *see* anything noble in your action.

100. ✗ I have decided to *cell* my property.

✔ I have decided to *sell* my property.

101. ✗ The accused will be kept in the *sell.*

✔ The accused will be kept in the *cell.*

102. ✗ I *scent* a greeting to my friend.

✔ I *sent* a greeting to my friend.

103. ✗ Some people don't like applying *sent* to body.

✔ Some people don't like applying *scent* to body.

104. ✗ These mangoes are *sore.*

✔ These mangoes are *sour.*

105. ✗ This kite will *sour* high.

✔ This kite will *soar* high.

106. ✗ I have a *soar* throat.

✔ I have a *sore* throat.

107. ✗ The sun is *stationery.*

✔ The sun is *stationary.*

108. ✗ He owns a *stationary* shop.

✔ He owns a *stationery* shop.

109. ✗ This man is likely to *steel* your money.

✔ This man is likely to *steal* your money.

110. ✗ His heart is made of *steal.*

✔ His heart is made of *steel.*

111. ✗ Don't *temper* with this equipment.

✔ Don't *tamper* with this equipment.

112. ✗ He has a pleasing *tamper.*

✔ He has a pleasing *temper.*

113. ✗ He has been included in the *teem.*

✔ He has been included in the *team.*

114. ✗ This pond *teams* with mosquitoes.

✔ This pond *teems* with mosquitoes.

115. ✗ You can park your car *their.*

✔ You can park your car *there.*

116. ✗ I don't like *there* behaviour.

✔ I don't like *their* behaviour.

117. ✗ The *king* sat on the thrown.

✔ The *king* sat on the throne.

118. ✗ I have *throne* the rubbish in the dustbin.

✔ I have *thrown* the rubbish in the dust bin.

119. ✘ The nightingale burst her *vain* and died.

✔ The nightingale burst her *vein* and died.

120. ✘ All my efforts to persuade him were in *vein.*

✔ All my efforts to persuade him were in *vain.*

121. ✘ He has written many *worses* in English.

✔ He has written many *verses* in English.

122. ✘ Your handwriting is *verse* than that of your colleague.

✔ Your handwriting is *worse* than that of your colleague.

123. ✘ We should not *veil* for the dead.

✔ We should not *wail* for the dead.

124. ✘ Muslim women wear *wail* to cover their head.

✔ Muslim women wear *veil* to cover their head.

125. ✘ You need not *weight* for me.

✔ You need not *wait* for me.

126. ✘ He has gained *wait.*

✔ He has gained *weight.*

127. ✘ He had to *wonder* from place to place.

✔ He had to *wander* from place to place.

128. ✘ He will *wander* over your achievement.

✔ He will *wonder* over your achievement.

129. ✘ He met me on the *weigh.*

✔ He met me on the *way.*

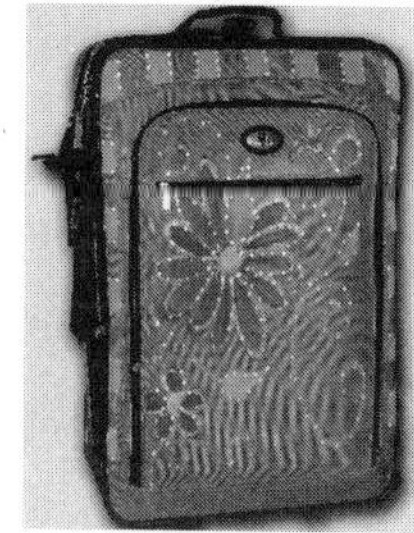

130. ✘ Please *way* the luggage.

✔ Please *weigh* this luggage.

131. ✘ We should honour the *cannons* of morality.

✔ We should honour the *canons* of morality.

132. ✘ The *corpse* of a cow was lying on the road.

✔ The *carcass* of a cow was lying on the road.

133. ✘ The *carcass* of a street beggar was carried to the burial ground.

✔ The *corpse* of a street beggar was carried to the burial ground.

134. ✘ The *monitor* of my computer is deficient.

✔ The *monitor* of my computer is defective.

135. ✘ She is *defective* in *politeness.*

✔ She is *deficient* in *politeness.*

136. ✘ The old man is *deceased.*

✔ The old man is *diseased.*

137. ✘ His *diseased* father left a lot of property.

✔ His *deceased* father left a lot of property.

138. ✘ My *oldest* brother is an engineer.

✔ My *eldest* brother is an engineer.

139. ✘ This woman is the *eldest* person in this village.

✔ This woman is the *oldest* person in this village.

140. ✘ He has applied for an *immigration* visa to Australia.

✔ He has applied for an *emigration* visa to Australia.

141. ✘ *Emigration* of Americans to India is likely to increase.

✔ *Immigration* of Americans to India is likely to increase.

142. ✘ Mahatma Gandhi was an *imminent* leader.

✔ Mahatma Gandhi was an *eminent* leader.

143. ✘ Demolition of this structure is *eminent.*

✔ Demolition of this structure is *imminent.*

144. ✘ He lives *further* from this place.

✔ He lives *farther* from this place.

145. ✘ The teacher asked the student to read *farther*.

✔ The teacher asked the student to read *further*.

146. ✘ In order to achieve success you must work *hardly*.

✔ In order to achieve success you must work *hard*.

147. ✘ He *hard* comes to my house these days.

✔ He *hardly* comes to my house these days.

148. ✘ We must help our fellow *humane* beings.

✔ We must help our fellow *human* beings.

149. ✘ He possesses great *human* qualities.

✔ He possesses great *humane* qualities.

150. ✘ He is *ingenuous* at inventing things.

✔ He is *ingenious* at inventing things.

151. ✘ All admire him because of his *ingenious* nature.

✔ All admire him because of his *ingenuous* nature.

152. ✘ My father *exceeded* to my request.

✔ My father *acceded* to my request.

153. ✘ In this city you are not allowed to *accede* the speed limit.

✔ In this city you are not allowed to *exceed* the speed limit.

154. ✘ The desire to possess more will lead to *edition* of troubles.

✔ The desire to possess more will lead to *addition* of troubles.

155. ✘ This is the latest *addition* of this book.

✔ This is the latest *edition* of this book.

156. ✘ The authors have made many *illusions* to the Bible.

✔ The authors have made many *allusions* to the Bible.

157. ✘ You should not live under the *allusion* that money can buy everything.

✔ You should not live under the *illusion* that money can buy everything.

158. ✘ Your remarks are not *opposite* to the occasion.

✔ Your remarks are not *apposite* to the occasion.

159. ✘ There is a restaurant *apposite* to my house.

✔ There is a restaurant *opposite* to my house.

160. ✘ Overwork will *ale* you

✔ Overwork will *ail* you.

161. ✘ I don't like drinking *ail*.

✔ I don't like drinking *ale*.

CLUES

1. Accept-consent to receive (a thing offered)
2. Except-(not including).
3. Access-(approach).
4. Excess-(in the state or an instance of exceeding).
5. Adapt-(to adjust).
6. Adopt-(to follow).
7. Adept-(expert in something).
8. Advice- (counsel-Noun).
9. Advise- (to give advice-Verb)
10. Affect- (produce an effect upon).
11. Effect- ((i) the result or consequence of an action (ii) to bring about.)

12. Air-(mixture of gases).
13. Heir- (one who inherits property)
14. Altar-(a place where religious rites are performed)
15. Alter-to change
16. Angel- (a messenger from heaven).
17. Angle- (a point where two straight lines meet).
18. Bear- ((i)to tolerate, (ii) a kind of animal).
19. Bare- (naked).
20. Beer- (a kind of wine).
21. Berth- (a sleeping place in a train).
22. Birth- (the emergence of a fully developed infant or other young from the body of its mother).
23. Born- (took birth).
24. Borne-(Past participle of the verb 'bear').
25. Brake-(an appliance for lessening the speed of a vehicle).
26. Break-(to make into pieces).
27. Bridal-(belonging to a bride).
28. Bridle- (the head gear of a horse).
29. Canvas- (a cloth of temp, flax or cotton).
30. Canvass- (to solicit or ask for votes).
31. Check- (to stop, to verify).
32. Cheque- (a bank slip for payment of money).
33. Ceiling- (top surface of the room).
34. Scaling- (to stamp with scal).
35. Complement- (something that completes).
36. Compliments- (regards, respect, greetings).
37. Council- (an assembly of persons).
38. Counsel- (advice).
39. Course- (path, progress, syllabus).

40. Dear- (beloved).
41. Deer- (a kind of stag).
42. Dose- (quantity of medicine taken at a time).
43. Doze- (to sleep lightly).
44. Fair–(just, beautiful a periodical market).
45. Fare- (the price a passenger has to pay to be conveyed by bus train etc).
46. Floor-(ground, lower surface of the room).
47. Flour-(the finely ground powder).
48. Fright-(a sudden fear).
49. Freight-(hire charges).
50. Gilt-(overlaid with gold).
51. Guilt-(sin, crime).
52. Goal-(aim).
53. Gaol-(jail, prison).

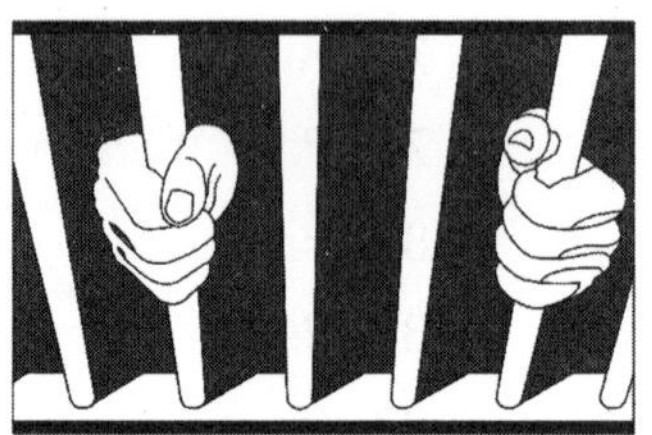

54. Hair-(thread like growing on the head).
55. Hare-(a kind of quadruped animal).
56. Heir-(successor).
57. Hale- (healthy).
58. Hail-(frozen rain, take birth from, praise).
59. Heal-(to make healthy).
60. Heel-(the hinder part of the foot).
61. Hole-(an empty space in a solid body).
62. Whole-(complete).
63. Insight- (perception, deep study).
64. Incite- (to urge on, to provoke, to anger).
65. Later- (afterwards, late in time).
66. Latter- (the second of the two, next).
67. Lose- (to be deprived of).

68. Loose- (not tight).
69. Meddle- (to interfere)
70. Medal-(an award in the form of a metallic coin).
71. Minor- (underaged person, small or simple).
72. Miner- (one who works in a mine).
73. Naughty- (wicked).
74. Knotty- (difficult).
75. None- (not any-Pronoun).
76. Nun- (a woman monk).
77. Order-(a command)
78. Ardour-(zeal)
79. Pair- (two things).
80. Pare- (cut into slices).
81. Pear- (fleshy sweet fruit).

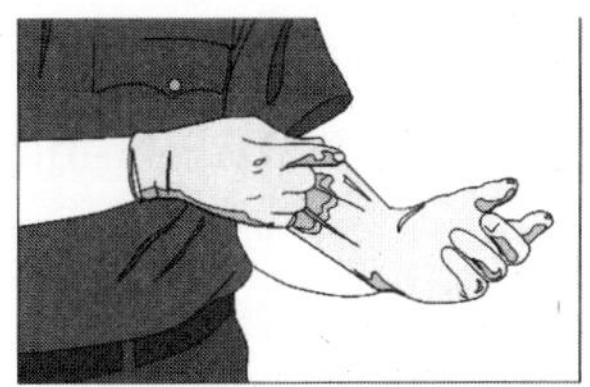

Pair of Gloves

82. Piece- (a bit).
83. Peace- (calmness).
84. Pray- (make devout supplication, entreat).
85. Prey- (a victim).
86. Principal- (the head of school, college or university).
87. Prophet- (founder of a religion, a teacher or interpreter of the supposed will of God).
88. Profit- (gain).
89. Quite- (completely).
90. Quiet- (calm).
91. Root- (the part of a plant under the ground).
92. Rout- (to defeat).
93. Route-(way, path).
94. Riot-(uproar, public disorder).
95. Ryot-(an Indian peasant).

96. See-(discern by use of eyes, observe, look at).
97. Sea-(ocean).
98. Cell-(a small room especially in a prison).
99. Sent-(past tense of the verb 'send').

100. Scent-(perfume).
101. Soar- (to rise).
102. Sour- (bitter).
103. Sore- (a painful growth in the body).
104. Stationary- (static, still).
105. Stationery- (writing materials etc. sold by a stationer).

106. Steal- (the act of stealing).
107. Steel- (iron).
108. Tamper- (to meddle, to spoil).
109. Temper- (disposition, mood).
110. Team- (a group of players).
111. Teem- (fill with, abound).
112. There- (at that place or position-Adverb).
113. Their- (belonging to them).
114. Throne- (the seat of a ruler).
115. Thrown- (past participle of the verb 'throw').
116. Vein- (a blood vessel).
117. In vain- (without result)
118. Verse- (a poem).
119. Worse- (comparative degree of 'bad').
120. Wail- (to weep, to cry in sorrow).
121. Veil- (a piece of fabric to conceal the face).

122. Wait- (postpone action or departure for a specified time).

123. Weight- (the heaviness of a body).

124. Wander- (move or hang about in particular area).

125. Wonder- (surprise).

126. Weigh- (find the weight of).

127. Way- (passage).

128. Cannon- (a heavy gun).

129. Canon- (a rule or principle).

130. Carcass- (the dead body of an animal).

131. Corpse- (the dead body of a human being).

132. Defective- (having some defect).

133. Deficient- (insufficient).

134. Diseased- (sick).

135. Deceased- (a dead person).

136. Eldest- (first born).

137. Oldest- (most advanced in age).

138. Emigration- (going out of a country).

139. Immigration- (coming into a country).

140. Eminent- (distinguished, notable).

141. Imminent- (about to happen).

142. Farther- (refers to distance).

143. Further- (additional).

144. Hardly- (scarcely).

145. Hard- (stenuously).

146. Human- (belonging to the genus Homo).

147. Humane- (compassionate, benevolent).

148. Ingenuous- (frank and innocent).
149. Ingenious- (clever).
150. Acceded to- (agreed to).
151. Exceed- (surpass, excel).
152. Addition- (the act or process of adding).
153. Edition- (one of the particular forms in which a literary work is published).
154. Allusions- (an indirect reference).
155. Illusion- (a deceptive appearance, false notion).
156. Apposite- (relevant, proper).
157. Opposite- (contrary, against, in front of).
158. Ail- (to be ill).
159. Ale- (beer).

15

Spelling Errors

English not being a phonetic language, English spellings are often confusing, complex and perplexing. Besides, the writing of letters in words do not conform to pronunciation. The confusion is further compounded because there is hardly any language dead or alive from which English has not liberally borrowed.

Most of common spelling errors are attributed to distaste for spellings and careless observation of the order of letters in a given word. However, one can create an order out of this seeming disorder of English spellings by patience, perseverance, practice and will to improve.

A few examples of common errors of spellings are given below:

1. ✘ There is *posibility* of his recovery.
   ✔ There is *possibility* of his recovery.
2. ✘ He had to work *throuout* the night.
   ✔ He had to work *throughout* the night.
3. ✘ Practice makes a man *prefect.*
   ✔ Practice makes a man *perfect.*
4. ✘ *Plow* is an *impliment* used in farming.
   ✔ *Plough* is an *implement* used in farming.

5. ✗ You should take part in *extra-curricullar* activities.
   ✓ You should take part in *extra curricular* activities.
6. ✗ He does not like *coffe.*
   ✓ He does not like *coffee.*

7. ✗ This post is *temparary.*
   ✓ This post is *temporary.*
8. ✗ He was elected *unanimusly.*
   ✓ He was elected *unanimously.*
9. ✗ I am a member of this *assosiation.*
   ✓ I am a member of this *association.*
10. ✗ Man being a social animal lives in a *socity.*
    ✓ Man being a social animal lives in *society.*
11. ✗ This office has been set up with a forign *colaboration.*
    ✓ This office has been set up with a foreign *collaboration.*
12. ✗ You should *encurge* your son to improve his grammar.
    ✓ You should *encourage* your son to improve his grammar.
13. ✗ Many students are weak in English *grammer.*
    ✓ Many students are weak in English *grammar.*
14. ✗ He has become old and *week.*
    ✓ He has become old and *weak.*
15. ✗ The matter will be *discused* thoroughly.
    ✓ The matter will be *discussed* thoroughly.
16. ✗ He enjoys *partisipating* in debates.
    ✓ He enjoys *participating* in debates.
17. ✗ *Libraris* will remain closed tomorrow.

✔ *Libraries* will remain closed tomorrow.

18. ✘ He is not the member of this *committe.*

✔ He is not the member of this *committee.*

19. ✘ The authorities are trying to explore new *avenews* of knowledge.

✔ The authorities are trying to explore new *avenues* of knowledge.

20. ✘ The players have entered the *pavillion.*

✔ The players have entered the *pavilion.*

21. ✘ It was an *inaugral* function.

✔ It was an *inaugural* function.

22. ✘ The students gave *diferent* answers.

✔ The students gave *different* answers.

23. ✘ The *goverment* schools will remain closed tomorrow.

✔ The *government* schools will remain closed tomorrow.

24. ✘ Your *performence* has improved considerably.

✔ Your *performance* has improved considerably.

25. ✘ Keep these 'items *seperately.*

✔ Keep these items *separately.*

26. ✘ I am not *intrested* in such activities.

✔ I am not *interested* in such activities.

27. ✘ You should help him in all *circamstances.*

✔ You should help him in all *circumstances.*

28. ✘ The Mugals were prepared to face the *agression.*

✔ The Mugals were prepared to face the *aggression.*

29. ✘ It was a *colosal* task to defeat the enemy forces in Kargil War.

✔ It was a *colossal* task to defeat the enemy forces in Kargil War.

30. ✘ The date of his *marrige* has been postponed.

    ✔ The date of his *marriage* has been postponed.

31. ✘ What is your *hoby* ?

    ✔ What is your *hobby* ?

32. ✘ His hobby is *gardning*.

    ✔ His hobby is *gardening*.

33. ✘ There is a large *varity* of items available here.

    ✔ There is a large *variety* of items available here.

34. ✘ We must make *vigourous* efforts to unite under one banner.

    ✔ We must make *vigorous* efforts to unite under one banner.

35. ✘ He narrated a *humourous* incident.

    ✔ He narrated to *humorous* incident.

36. ✘ The story does not *potray* anything new.

    ✔ This story does not *portray* anything new.

37. ✘ You should *vaccate* this house immediately.

    ✔ You should *vacate* this house immediately.

38. ✘ Everyone of us should have *petriotic* feelings for our country.

✔ Everyone of us should have *patriotic* feelings for our country.

39. ✘ Don't have *enemity* with anyone.

✔ Don't have *enmity* with any one.

40. ✘ The soldiers fought *bravly.*

✔ The soldiers fought *bravely.*

41. ✘ His house is near the *mosqe.*

✔ His house is near the *mosque.*

42. ✘ He is *earstwhile* prince of Mebar.

✔ He is *erstwhile* prince of Mebar.

43. ✘ Your *credibillity* has been eroded.

✔ Your *credibility* has been eroded.

44. ✘ She has gone to a *forein* country.

✔ She has gone to a *foreign* country.

45. ✘ You must *eppriciate* the good work done by others.

✔ You must *appreciate* the good work done by others.

46. ✘ *Finaly* we succeeded in our objective.

✔ *Finally* we succeeded in our objective.

47. ✘ The UPA *Parliamentry* party is in session.

✔ The UPA *Parliamentary* party is in session.

48. ✘ Every one should *condem* the terrorist attacks.

✔ Every one should *condemn* the terrorist attacks.

49. ✘ All the *passengars* were asked to get down the bus.

✔ All the *passengers* were asked to get down the bus.

50. ✗ The *carfew* has been lifted.

✔ The *curfew* has been lifted.

51. ✗ Do you have the new telephone *directry*?

✔ Do you have the new telephone *directory*?

52. ✗ This is an *abrigement* of the first edition.

✔ This is an *abridgement* of the first edition.

53. ✗ Can you *accomodate* a few more persons?

✔ Can you *accommodate* a few more persons?

54. ✗ *Apperances* may be deceptive.

✔ *Appearances* may be deceptive.

55. ✗ He gave me a sound *advise*.

✔ He gave me a sound *advice*.

56. ✗ He will *advice* you sincerely.

✔ He will *advise* you sincerely.

57. ✗ Don't mishandle the *appratus*.

✔ Don't mishandle the *apparatus*.

58. ✗ What is your *assesment* of this person?

✔ What is your *assessment* of this person?

59. ✗ We are *approching* the airport.

✔ We are *approaching* the airport.

60. ✗ I am not *accastomed* to such a climate.

✔ I am not *accustomed* to such a climate.

61. ✗ This medicine benefitted me a lot.

✔ This medicine benefited me a lot.

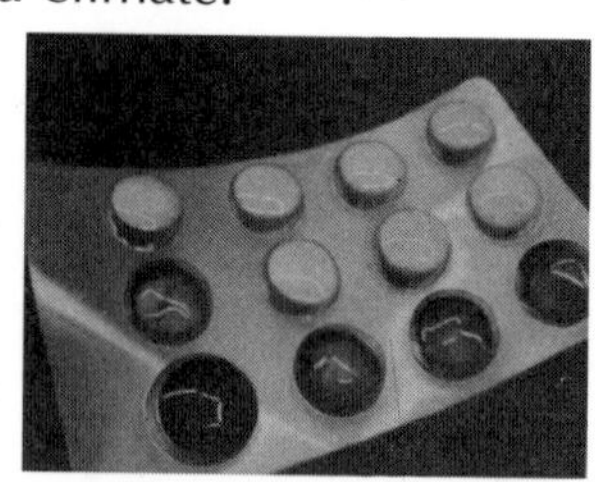

62. ✗ Where is your *bycycle*?

✔ Where is your *bicycle*?

63. ✘ We should love our *brethern*.

✔ We should love our *brethren*.

64. ✘ I shall meet you in *brake*.

✔ I shall meet you in *break*.

65. ✘ The *break* of my car is not working properly.

✔ The *brake* of my car is not working properly.

66. ✘ He is not the member of this *burou*.

✔ He is not the member of this *bureau*.

67. ✘ We are not allowed to cross the *boundry*.

✔ We are not allowed to cross the *boundary*.

68. ✘ Can you give me a new *calender*?

✔ Can you give me a new *calendar*?

69. ✘ He has *choosen* the clothes of his choice.

✔ He has *chosen* the clothes of his choice.

70. ✘ They were wearing *course* clothes.

✔ They were wearing *coarse* clothes.

71. ✘ He left the place *immediatly*.

✔ He left the place *immediately*.

72. ✘ There are *miscelleneous* exercises in this book.

✔ There are *miscellaneous* exercises in this book.

Below is given a comprehensive list of words generally mis-spelled:

Commonly Mis-spelled Words

A

Abate
Abbreviate
Abdicate
Abduction
Abhor
Abject
Abominable
Aboriginal
Abridge
Absolve
Absorb
Abundant
Accede
Accessible
Accessory
Accolade
Accommodate
Accomplice
Accord
Accost
Accrue
Acknowledge
Acrimonious
Acumen
Acute
Adamant
Addiction
Address
Adept

Adhere
Adjacent
Adulation
Adversary
Adversity
Aesthetic
Affable
Affected
Affidavit
Affiliation
Affinity
Affirmation
Aftermath
Agenda
Aggregate
Aggressor
Agility
Allay
Allege
Alleviate
Allocate
Allusion
Aloof
Amass
Ambiguous
Amend
Amenities
Amiable
Amicable

Amnesty
Analogy
Anarchy
Anguish
Animosity
Annihilate
Annul
Anomaly
Antecedents
Anthem
Arrears
Arrest
Arrogance
Aspire
Assail
Assert
Assumption
Assurance
Asteroid
Asylum
Attest
Attribute
Augment
Authoritarian
Autocratic
Automation
Auxiliary
Azure

B

Babble
Baffle
Bait
Balk
Balm
Bane
Barrage
Barricade
Bastion
Beguile
Belittle
Bellicose
Belligerent
Bemoan
Benediction
Benefactor
Beneficial
Benevolent
Benign
Bereft
Beseech
Beset
Besiege
Bestial
Bestow
Betray
Biennial
Billowing
Bizarre
Blatant
Bluff
Blunder
Bode
Bolster
Bombardment
Booming
Boon
Boycott
Brandish
Bravado
Breadth
Brevity
Bristling
Brittle
Brochure
Browse
Brunt
Buffet
Bungalow
Buoyant
Bureaucracy
Burly
Bustle
Buttress
Buxom

C

Cache
Cacophonous
Cadence
Cajole
Calculated
Calibre
Calligraphy
Callous
Camouflage
Canto
Canvass
Capacious
Capacity
Caprice
Captivate
Cardiologist
Carnage
Carnal
Carnivorous
Cascade
Castigate
Casualty
Catapult
Catastrophe
Celebrated
Censor
Censure
Centrifugal
Ceremonious
Cessation

Cession
Chafe
Chaff
Chagrin
Champion
Chaotic
Charisma
Chassis
Chaste
Check
Chequered
Chicanery
Chide
Chisel
Chronic
Cipher
Citadel
Cite
Clamber
Clandestine
Clasp
Clench
Cloister
Coalition
Coercion
Cohere
Coincidence
Collaborate
Colloquial
Collusion
Colossal
Commemorate
Communal
Compatible
Compile
Complacency
Complementary
Compliance
Comprehensive
Comprise
Concede
Concerted
Concession
Conciliatory
Concise
Concord
Condemn
Condense
Condole
Condone
Conducive
Confidant
Confine
Confirm
Conformity
Congenial
Consensus
Consequential
Consign
Consistency
Conspiracy
Constraint
Consumate
Contemporary
Context
Converge
Conviction
Cordial
Correlation
Corrode
Countenance
Credibility
Culminate
Culvert
Curator
Cursory
Curtail

D

Dais
Dank
Dearth
Debacle
Debris
Decadence
Derivative
Dermatologist
Derogatory
Desecrate
Desolate
Despise
Destitute
Detergent
Deterrent

Detraction
Detrimental
Deviate
Devise
Devout
Diffidence
Diligence
Dilute
Din
Dint
Disband
Disburse
Disclaim
Discord
Discrepancy
Discretion
Discriminating
Disdain
Disfigure
Dishearten
Disinterested
Dislodge
Dismantle
Dismay

Dismember
Dismiss
Disparity
Dispassionate
Disperse
Dispirited
Dissection
Dissent
Dissident
Dissipate
Dissuade
Distant
Distill
Distinction
Distort
Divergent
Diverse
Diversion
Diversity
Divest
Divulge
Docile
Doctrinate

Document
Dogged
Dogmatic
Doldrums
Domicile
Domineer
Don
Dormant
Dossier
Dote
Douse
Downcast
Dregs
Drone
Dubious
Dumbfound
Dupe
Duplicity
Duration
Duress
Dutiful
Dwindle
Dynamic

E

Earthy
Ebb
Eccentric
Ecclesiastic
Eclipse
Ecologist
Economy

Ecstasy
Edict
Edify
Eerie
Efface
Efficacy
Effigy

Egoism
Elated
Elegy
Elicit
Elixir
Elucidate
Elusive

Emaciated
Emanate
Embargo
Embellish
Embezzlement
Embody
Embrace
Embroider
Eminent
Emissary
Empathy
Emulate
Enclave
Encompass
Encroachment
Endearment
Endemic
Endorse
Engender
Enigma
Enmity
Entail
Enterprising
Enthrall
Entice
Entitlement
Entity
Entrance
Entrepreneur
Ephemeral
Epic
Epigram
Epitaph
Epitome
Equilibrium
Equitable
Equivocal
Erode
Erratic
Erroneous
Erudite
Escapism
Eschew
Esoteric
Espionage
Esteem
Ethnic
Ethos
Evasive
Evince
Exalt
Excerpt
Excise
Execute
Exemplary
Exempt
Exertion
Exhaustive
Exhilarating
Exhort
Exhume
Exigency
Exodus
Exonerate
Expedite
Explicit
Exposure
Expunge
Extent
Extol
Extrovert
Exude
Exult

F

Fabricate
Façade
Facet
Facile
Fallacious
Fallible
Fallow
Falter
Fancy
Fatalism
Fathom
Fauna
Feasible
Feign
Felicity
Ferment
Fervent
Fervour
Fickle
Fidelity
Figment

Filament
Finale
Fissure
Flagrant
Flair
Flamboyant
Flaunt
Fleece
Flinch
Flippant
Flora
Flounder
Flourish
Flout
Fluctuate
Fluency
Fluke
Fodder
Foliage
Foment
Foolhardy
Forbearance
Forebears
Foreboding
Foreshadow
Foresight
Forestall
Forgo
Forlorn
Formality
Formidable
Forsake
Forswear
Forte
Forthright
Fortitude
Fortuitous
Forum
Foster
Fracas
Frail
Franchise
Frantic
Fraudulent
Fraught
Fray
Frenzied
Fret
Friction
Frigid
Frivolous
Frugality
Frustrate
Fugitive
Furlough
Fusion
Futile

G

Gait
Galaxy
Gale
Gall
Galleon
Gambol
Gamely
Gamut
Gape
Garish
Garner
Garnish
Garrulous
Gaudy
Gaunt
Genealogy
Generate
Generic
Genesis
Genre
Genteel
Gentry
Germane
Germinate
Gesticulation
Ghastly
Gingerly
Girth
Gist
Glaring
Glimmer
Gloat
Glossary
Glut
Glutton
Goad

Gorge
Gouge
Gourmet
Graduated
Graft
Grandeur
Grandiloquent
Grandiose
Graphic
Grapple
Grate
Gratify
Gratis
Gratuitous
Gravity
Gregarious
Grievance
Grill
Grimace
Grisly
Grouse
Grotesque
Grove
Grovel
Gruff
Guile
Gullible

H

Hackneyed
Haggard
Haggle
Hallucination
Hamper
Haphazard
Harass
Hardy
Harrowing
Haughtiness
Hazardous
Hazy
Headlong
Headstrong
Heckler
Hedonist
Heed
Heinous
Heresy
Hermitage
Heterogenous
Heyday
Hiatus
Hibernate
Hierarchy
Hindrance
Histrionic
Hoard
Hoary
Hoax
Hodgepodge
Homage
Homogenous
Hoodwink
Horde
Horticultural
Host
Hostility
Hovel
Hover
Hue
Humane
Humdrum
Humid
Humidity
Hurtle
Hybrid
Hydrophobia
Hyperbole
Hypercritical
Hypocritical
Hypothetical

I

Icon
Ideology
Idiom
Idiosyncrasy
Idolatory
Ignite
Ignoble
Ignominy
Illicit

Illuminate
Illusion
Illusory
Imbalance
Imbibe
Immaculate
Imminent
Immune
Immutable
Impart
Impartial
Impasse
Impeach
Impeccable
Impede
Impel
Impenetrable
Impending
Imperative
Imperious
Impetus
Impinge
Implacable
Implicate
Implication
Implicit
Imply
Impotant
Impoverished
Impregnable
Impromptu
Impudence
Impugn

Impunity
Inane
Inanimate
Inaugurate
Incarnation
Incentive
Inception
Incessant
Incipient
Incite
Inclement
Incongruous
Inconsistency
Incorporate
Incorrigible
Incredulous
Inculcate
Incursion
Indelible
Indices
Indifferent
Indigenous
Indisputable
Indoctrinate
Indolent
Indomitable
Induce
Industrious
Inebriated
Inept
Inevitable
Inexorable
Infallible

Infidel
Infiltrate
Infirmity
Inflated
Influx
Infuriate
Ingenious
Inherent
Inimical
Inquitous
Initiate
Inkling
Innate
Innocuous
Innovative
Inquisitor
Insalubrious
Insatiable
Insidious
Insinuate
Insipid
Insolvent
Insomnia
Insubordination
Insurgent
Insurmountable
Intangible
Intelligentsia
Inter
Interim
Intermittent
Intervene

Intimidate
Intrepid
Intricate
Intrinsic
Introvert
Invective
Invigorate
Invincible
Invocation
Iota
Ire
Irony
Irresolute
Irretrievable
Irreverence
Irrevocable
Itinerary

J

Jabber
Japed
Jargon
Jaundiced
Jaunt
Jeopardize
Jettison
Jingoist
Jocular
Jostle
Jovial
Jubilation
Judicious
Juncture
Junta
Jurisprudence
Justification

K

Keleidoscope
Kernel
Kindle
Kindred
Kinetic
Kleptomaniac
Knave
Knoll
Knotty
Kudos

L

Laborious
Labyrinth
Laceration
Lackadaisical
Laconic
Laggard
Lampoon
Languid
Languish
Larder
Lassitude
Latent
Lateral
Land
Lavish
Lax
Lechery
Leery
Legacy
Legend
Leniency
Lethal
Lethargic
Levity
Lewd
Liability
Liaison
Libel
Licentious
Lilliputian
Limber
Limpid
Lineage
Linger
Linguistic
Liquidate

Listless
Litany
Litigation
Livid
Loath
Loathe
Lofty
Log
Loiter
Longevity
Loom
Lucid
Lucrative
Ludicrous
Lugubrious
Lumber
Luminary
Luminous
Lunar
Lunge
Lurid
Luscious
Lustrous
Luxuriant

M

Magnanimous
Magnate
Magnitude
Maladroit
Malady
Malaise
Malcontent
Malefactor
Malevolent
Malicious
Malign
Malignant
Mammoth
Mandate
Mandatory
Manifesto
Manipulate
Marital
Maritime
Marred
Martial
Martyr
Materialism
Maverick
Meagre
Mediate
Mediocre
Melancholy
Membrane
Mercenary
Merger
Metamorphosis
Metaphysical
Meticulous
Metropolis
Migratory
Maritime
Milieu
Militant
Mimicry
Minuscule
Mirth
Misanthrope
Mishap
Misnomer
Missive
Mite
Mitigate
Mock
Modicum
Modulate
Mollify
Momentous
Moratorium
Morbid
Morose
Mosaic
Motif
Muddle
Multifaceted
Mundane
Murky
Muster
Mutability
Mutinous
Myopic

N

Nadir
Narcissist
Narrative
Nascent
Nauseate
Nautical
Nebulous
Nefarious
Negate
Negligible
Nemesis
Nepotism
Nicety
Nihilist
Nip
Nocturnal
Nomadic
Nomenclature
Nominal
Non chalance
Noncommittal
Nondescript
Nonplus
Nostalgia
Notoriety
Novelty
Novice
Nuance
Nullify
Numismatist
Nuptial
Nurture
Nutrient

O

Oaf
Obdurate
Obese
Obituary
Obligatory
Oblique
Obliterate
Oblivion
Oblivious
Obnoxious
Obscure
Obsequious
Obsessive
Obsolete
Obstinate
Obtrude
Obtuse
Obviate
Odious
Odium
Odorous
Odyssey
Offensive
Offhand
Officious
Ogle
Olfactory
Oligarchy
Ominous
Omnipotent
Omniscient
Omnivorous
Onerous
Onset
Onus
Opaque
Opportunist
Optimist
Optimum
Optional
Opulence
Orator
Ordain
Ordeal
Ordinance
Orgy
Orient
Ornithologist
Oscillate
Ostensible
Ostracize
Oust
Outmoded
Outskirts
Outspoken
Outstrip
Outwit

Ovation
Overbearing
Overt
Overwrought

P

Pacifist
Pacify
Paean
Palatable
Pall
Palliate
Pallid
Palpable
Paltry
Panacea
Panache
Pandemonium
Pander
Panoramic
Parable
Paradigm
Paradox
Paragon
Parallelism
Paramount
Paraphernalia
Parasite
Parched
Pariah
Parity
Parochial
Parody
Parsimony
Partial
Partisan
Pastoral
Pathetic
Pathological
Pathos
Patriarch
Patronize
Paucity
Pauper
Pecuniary
Pedagogy
Pedant
Peerless
Pejorative
Penchant
Pendant
Pensive
Penury
Perceptive
Peremptory
Perennial
Perfunctory
Peripheral
Perjury
Permeable
Permeate
Pernicious
Perpetrate
Perpetuate
Pertinent
Perturb
Peruse
Phenomena
Philanderer
Philanthropist
Phobia
Phoenix
Piety
Pillage
Pithy
Pittance
Pivotal
Placate
Placid
Plaintive
Plausible
Plethora
Plight
Plumb
Plumage
Poignancy
Porous
Posthumous
Posterity
Postulate
Potable
Potent
Pragmatic
Prank
Prattle
Preamble

Precedent
Precept
Precinct
Precipitate
Preclude
Precursor
Predator
Predicament
Preempt
Prelude
Premeditate
Premise
Premonition
Preposterous
Prerogative
Pretentious
Pretext
Prey
Pristine
Privation
Problematic
Prod
Prodigal
Prodigious
Prodigy
Profusion
Progeny
Projectile
Proliferation
Prolific
Prologue
Promiscuous
Promulgate
Propagate
Prophetic
Propitiate
Propitious
Proponent
Propriety
Prosaic
Proscribe
Prostrate
Protégé
Protocol
Prototype
Protract
Protrude
Provident
Provisional
Provoke
Proximity
Prudent
Pseudonym
Psyche
Purile
Pugnacity
Punctilious
Pungent
Punitive
Purge
Purported
Purveyor
Putrid
Pyromaniac

Q

Quack
Quadruped
Quagmire
Quaint
Quandary
Quarantine
Quarry
Quay
Quell
Quench
Query
Quibble
Quiescent
Quintessence
Quip
Quirk
Quiver
Quixotic
Quizzical
Quorum

R

Rabid
Rail
Rally
Ramble
Ramification
Ramp

Rampant
Ramshackle
Random
Rant
Rapacious
Rapport
Rapt
Ratify
Rationale
Raucous
Rave
Ravel
Ravenous
Raze
Realm
Rebuff
Rebuke
Rebuttal
Recapitulate
Recession
Recipient
Reciprocal
Recluse
Reconcile
Reconnaissance
Recourse
Rectify
Recurrent
Redress
Redundant
Refrain
Refurbish
Refute
Regale

Regime
Rehabilitate
Reimburse
Reiterate
Rejoinder
Rejuvenate
Relegate
Relic
Relinquish
Relish
Remission
Remorse
Renounce
Renovate
Reparation
Repast
Repeal
Repercussion
Replenish
Replete
Replica
Reprehensive
Repress
Reprieve
Reprimand
Reprisal
Reproach
Reprove
Repugnant
Requisite
Rescind
Residue
Resolution
Resonant

Respite
Resplendid
Restraint
Resumption
Resurge
Retaliation
Retentive
Retinue
Retort
Retract
Retrench
Retribution
Retrieve
Retrograde
Retrospective
Revelry
Reverent
Revoke
Revulsion
Rhetoric
Riddle
Rife
Rigorous
Rivulet
Robust
Rostrum
Rout
Rubble
Rudimentary
Ruffian
Ruminate
Rummage
Rustic
Ruthless

S

Saboteur
Sacrilegious
Sacrosanct
Sadistic
Saga
Salient
Salubrious
Salutary
Salvage
Salvo
Sanctimonious
Sanctuary
Sanguine
Sap
Sarcasm
Sardonic
Satiate
Satire
Saturate
Saunter
Scabbard
Scanty
Scapegoat
Scavenge
Scenario
Schism
Scintillate
Scoff
Scrutinize
Scuffle
Scurry
Seamy
Seasoned
Seclusion
Sectarian
Sedentary
Sedition
Seemly
Seethe
Sensual
Sentinel
Serenity
Serpentine
Servile
Sever
Shakle
Sham
Shambles
Sheathe
Shimmer
Shirk
Shoddy
Shun
Sibling
Simian
Simile
Simulate
Sinister
Skeptic
Skirmish
Slacken
Slander
Slothful
Slovenly
Sluggish
Smirk
Sobriety
Sojourn
Solace
Solemnity
Solicit
Soliloquy
Solitude
Solvent
Sonorous
Sordid
Sparse
Spate
Spawn
Spendthrift
Spontaneity
Sporadic
Spurious
Spurn
Squabble
Squander
Stagnant
Stalemate
Stalwart
Static
Statute
Steadfast
Stereotype
Stifle
Stigma
Stint

Stipulate
Stricture
Strident
Stringent
Stupor
Subdued
Subjective
Subjugate
Sublime
Submissive
Subservient
Subside
Subsistence
Substantial
Substantiate
Subversive
Succinct
Succulent
Sully
Summit
Superfluous
Superimpose
Supersede
Supple
Surfeit
Surly
Surmise
Surreptitious
Surrogate
Surveillance
Susceptible
Sustain
Sustenance
Swagger
Swerve
Sycophant
Symmetry
Synoptic
Synthesis

T

Tactile
Taint
Talesman
Tangible
Tanner
Tantelize
Tantrum
Tarry
Taut
Temperate
Tempo
Temporal
Tenacious
Tenet
Tentative
Tenuous
Terminology
Terminus
Terrestrial
Terse
Tether
Theocracy
Theoretical
Thespian
Threadbare
Thrive
Throes
Throng
Thwart
Timidity
Timorous
Tirade
Titanic
Topography
Torpor
Torrid
Torso
Tortuous
Totter
Touchy
Toxic
Trajectory
Tranquillity
Transcendent
Transcribe
Transgression
Transient
Transition
Transitory
Transparent
Trappings
Traumatic
Travail
Traverse

Treatise
Tremor
Trepidation
Trifling
Trivial
Tumult
Turbulence
Turmoil
Turncoat
Turpitude
Tutelage
Tycoon
Typhoon
Tyranny

U

Ubiquitous
Ulterior
Ultimate
Unanimity
Unassailable
Unassuming
Unbridled
Uncanny
Uncouth
Unctuous
Undermine
Underscore
Undulating
Unearth
Unequivocal
Unfathomable
Unfetter
Unfrock
Unimpeachable
Unintimidating
Unique
Unkempt
Unmitigated
Unobtrusive
Unpalatable
Unprecedented
Unravel
Unruly
Unscathed
Unseemly
Untenable
Unwarranted
Unwieldy
Unwitting
Upbraid
Uprorious
Upshot
Urbane
Usurp

V

Vacillate
Vagabond
Vagrant
Valedictory
Validate
Valour
Vampire
Vanguard
Vantage
Variegated
Vehement
Venal
Vendetta
Veneer
Venerable
Venerate
Venial
Venom
Vent
Veracity
Verbatim
Verbose
Verdant
Verge
Verisimilitude
Vernacular
Versatile
Verve
Vex
Viable
Vicissitude
Vie
Vigilance
Vigour
Vilify
Vindicate

Viper
Virtual
Virulent
Virus
Vital
Vitriolic
Vivacious
Vociferous
Vogue
Volatile
Voluble
Voracious
Vouchsafe
Vulnerable

W

Waffle
Waft
Waif
Waive
Wallow
Wane
Wanton
Warrant
Wary
Watershed
Wax
Waylay
Wean
Welter
Wheedle
Whelp
Whet
Whiff
Whimsical
Whinny
Willful
Wily
Wince
Windfall
Winnow
Wispy
Wistful
Witter
Withhold
Withstand
Witticism
Wizardry
Woe
Wrath
Wrench
Writhe
Wry

X

Xenophobia

Y

Yen
Yield
Yoke
Yore

Z

Zany
Zeal
Zealot
Zenith
Zephyr

16

Wrong Question Tags and Short Answers

It is a common practice in conversation to make a statement and ask for confirmation; as.

It's very hot, isn't it? The later part (isn't it?) is called Question Tag. The subject of the Question Tag is always a Pronoun, never a Noun. Study the following pattern to understand the correct use of Question Tags and Short Answers.

1. ✘ It's raining, is it?
   ✔ It's raining, isn't it?
2. ✘ John is free, is he?
   ✔ John is free, isn't he?
3. ✘ You can swim well, can you?
   ✔ You can swim well, can't you?
4. ✘ Darcy broke the cup, did he?
   ✔ Darcy broke the cup, did n't he?
5. ✘ Your wife cooks well, does she?
   ✔ Your wife cooks well, doesn't she?
6. ✘ She isn't busy, isn't she?
   ✔ She isn't busy, is she?

7. ✘ You can't swim, can't you?

✔ You can't swim, can you?

8. ✘ Joseph doesn't work hard, doesn't he?

✔ Joseph doesn't work hard, does he?

9. ✘ The guests havn't come yet, havn't they?

✔ The guests havn't come yet, have they?

CLUES

(i) It is a common practice in conversation to make a statement and ask for confirmation, as, It is very cold, isn't it? The later part (isn't it?) is called a Question Tag.

(ii) The pattern to be observed is — auxiliary + nt + subject, if the statement is positive — auxiliary + subject, if the statement is negative.

10.	Are you going abroad?	Yes, I am not.	
		No, I am.	✘
	Are you going abroad?	Yes, I am.	
		No, I am not.	✔
11.	Can you drive a mobike?	Yes, I can't.	
		No, I can.	✘
	Can you drive a mobike?	Yes, I can.	
		No, I can't.	✔
12.	Is your daughter married?	Yes, she is n't.	
		No, she is.	✘
	Is your daughter married?	Yes, she is.	
		No, she isn't.	✔

13. Do you play cricket?	Yes, I don't.	
	No, I do.	✘
Do you play cricket?	Yes, I do.	
	No, I don't.	✔
14. Did you say anything?	Yes, Ididn't.	
	No, I did.	✘
Did you say anything?	Yes, I did.	
	No, I didn't.	✔
15. Can you swim?	Yes, I can't.	
	No, I can.	✘
Can you swim?	Yes, I can.	
	No, I can't.	✔
16. Do you like sweets?	Yes, I don't.	
	No, I do.	✘
Do you like sweets?	Yes, I do.	
	No, I don't.	✔
17. Did you go to school yesterday?	Yes, I didn't.	
	No, I did.	✘
Did you go to school yesterday?	Yes, I did.	
	No, I didn't.	✔
18. Is John staying with his aunt?	Yes, He isn't.	
	No, he is.	✘
Is John staying with his aunt?	Yes, he is.	
	No, he isn't.	✔
19. Did you meet the examiner?	Yes, I didn't.	
	No, I did.	✘
Did you meet the examiner?	Yes, I did.	
	No, I didn't.	✔
20. Do you like oranges?	Yes, I don't.	
	No, I do.	✘

Do you like oranges? Yes, I do.
No, I don't. ✔

CLUES

The most usual form of short answers to verbal questions (i.e., questions beginning with an auxiliary) is:

(i) Yes + pronoun + auxiliary

or (ii) No + pronoun + auxiliary + n't (not).

21. ✘ It is a good book. Yes, the book is.
    ✔ It is a good book. Yes, it is.
22. ✘ John has already gone. So, John has.
    ✔ John has already gone. So, he has.
23. ✘ She can speak French very well. Of course, she can't.
    ✔ She can speak French very well. Of course, she can.
24. ✘ He looks dishonest. Yes, he looks.
    ✔ He looks dishonest. Yes, he does.

CLUES

Agreements with affirmative statements are made with yes/so/of course + pronoun + auxiliary.

25. ✘ The oranges aren't good. Yes, they aren't.
    ✔ The oranges aren't good. No, they aren't.
26. ✘ He does not like beef. Yes, he doesn't.
    ✔ He does not like beef. No, he doesn't.
27. ✘ She can't help laughing. Yes, she can't.
    ✔ She can't help laughing. No, she can't.
28. ✘ They have not acted well. Yes, they havn't.
    ✔ They have not acted well. No, they haven't.

CLUES

Agreements with Negative statements are made with No + pronoun + auxiliary + n't/not

29. ✗ She won't come here. Yes, she will.
    ✔ She won't come here. But she will.
30. ✗ You don't know him. Oh no, I do.
    ✔ You don't know him. Oh yes, I do.
31. ✗ I didn't say it. Oh, but you said.
    ✔ I didn't say it. Oh, but you did.
32. ✗ You can't understand it. No, I can.
    ✔ You can't understand it. Yes, I can.

CLUES

Disagreements with Negative statements are made with (Oh) yes/(Oh) but + pronoun + auxiliary:

33. ✗ You are drunk. Yes, I amn't.
    ✔ You are drunk. No, I amn't.
34. ✗ You are joking. Oh no, I'm.
    ✔ You are joking. Oh no, I'm not.
35. ✗ Why did you beat him? Yes, I didn't.
    ✔ Why did you beat him? But, I didn't.
36. ✗ I suppose he knows French. Yes, he doesn't.
    ✔ I suppose he knows French. But he doesn't.

CLUES

(i) Disagreements with affirmative statements are made with No/Oh no + pronoun + auxiliary + n't / not.

(ii) 'But' is used in disagreement with a question, or an assumption.

37. ✗ You must go home. So I must.
    ✔ You must go home. So must I.

37. ✘ John likes mangoes. So I do.

✔ John likes mangoes. So do I.

39. ✘ She was late for the meeting. So you were.

✔ She was late for the meeting. So were you.

40. ✘ I have completed my work. So my friend has.

✔ I have completed my work. So has my friend.

CLUES

Affirmative additions to affirmative remarks are made with – So + auxiliary + subject:

41. ✘ Johnsy does not like mangoes. Nor I do.

✔ Johnsy does not like mangoes. Nor do I.

42. ✘ She did n't like it. Neither I did.

✔ She didn't like it. Neither did I.

43. ✘ I can't solve the sum. Nor my friend can.

✔ I can't solve the sum. Nor can my friend.

44. ✘ Harry is not present. Neither John is.

✔ Harry is not present. Neither is John.

CLUES

Negative additions to Negative remarks are made with Nor/ Neither + auxiliary + subject.

45. ✘ You know French. But I know not.

✔ You know French. But I don't.

46. ✘ He understood the question. So Johnsy didn't.

✔ He understood the question. But Johnsy didn't.

47. ✗ He knows how to drive. As his wife doesn't.

✔ He knows how to drive. But his wife doesn't.

48. ✗ I can play chess. As my sister can't.

✔ I can play chess. But my sister can't.

CLUES

Negative additions to affirmative remarks are made with – But + Subject + auxiliary + n't/ not:

49. ✗ You don't know her. But do I.

✔ You don't know her. But I do.

50. ✗ Sophia didn't see the match. But did Johnsy.

✔ Sophia didn't see the match. But Johnsy did.

51. ✗ You can't drive a car. But can I.

✔ You can't drive car. But I can.

52. ✗ I wasn't late. But were you.

✔ I wasn't late. But you were.

CLUES

Affirmative additions to negative remarks are made with –But + Subject + auxiliary.

17 MISCELLANEOUS

1. ✗ All the mother-in-laws are present here.
   ✓ All the mothers-in-law are present here.
2. ✗ The commander- in-chiefs have arrived.
   ✓ The commanders-in chief have arrived.
3. ✗ You can now call the maids servant.
   ✓ You can now call the maid servants.
4. ✗ He has bought two pairs of oxes.
   ✓ He has bought two pairs of oxen.
5. ✗ You should avoid such hanger-ons.
   ✓ You should avoid such hangers-on.

6. ✗ Don't give yourself air.
   ✓ Don't give yourself airs.
7. ✗ He has broken my scissor.
   ✓ He has broken my scissors.
8. ✗ Cattles are grazing in the field.
   ✓ Cattle are grazing in the field.

9. ✘ The culprit was put in fetter.
   ✔ The culprit was put in fetters.
10. ✘ With best compliment.
    ✔ With best compliments.
11. ✘ Himachal Pradesh is famous for its salubrious environ.
    ✔ Himachal Pradesh is famous for its salubrious environs.
12. ✘ Your hairs are becoming grey.
    ✔ Your hair is becoming grey.

13. ✘ He lives in a spacious premise.
    ✔ He lives in a spacious premises.
14. ✘ A male sparrow was hurt.
    ✔ A cock-sparrow was hurt.
15. ✘ Where is your female servant?
    ✔ Where is your maid servant?
16. ✘ She is a bachelor?
    ✔ She is a spinster?

17. ✘ She is a great female benefactor.
    ✔ She is a great benefactress.
18. ✘ He was bitten by a she-dog.
    ✔ He was bitten by a bitch.
19. ✘ He was hit by a female horse.
    ✔ He was bit by a mare.
20. ✘ I have caught a male fish.
    ✔ I have caught a milter.
21. ✘ There was a beautiful he-doe in the forest.
    ✔ There was a beautiful buck in the forest.

22. ✗ She is the patron of our federation.
✓ She is the patroness of our federation.

23. ✗ Darcy wanted to become a she-monk.
✓ Darcy wanted to become a nun.

24. ✗ He is one of my best friend.
✓ He is one of my best friends.

25. ✗ I and he are taking part in the concert.
✓ He and I are taking part in the concert.

26. ✗ You are as intelligent as me.
✓ You are as intelligent as I.

27. ✗ You did better than me.
✓ You did better than I.

28. ✗ None of them have paid the electricity bill.
✓ None of them has paid the electricity bill.

29. ✗ One should do his duty.
✓ One should do one's duty.

30. ✗ I, he and you will go out.
✓ You, he and I will go out.

31. ✗ Whom do you think was there?
✓ Who do you think was there?

32. ✗ Who did you meet in the market?
✓ Whom did you meet in the market?

33. ✗ The man who I know has left this place.
✓ The man whom I know has left the place.

34. ✗ We should all cooperate with each other.
✓ We should all cooperate with one another.

Notes

Notes

Notes